The Call Goes Out

from the Cetacean Nation

Interspecies Communication of Love & Wisdom

Messages from Whales, Dolphins, & Porpoises,

including Keiko, Star of the "Free Willy" Movies

Dianne Robbins

I CLAIM EARTH'S COPYRIGHT for these messages
on behalf of all Cetaceans.

Portions of this book were formerly published as
The Call Goes Out: Messages from the Earth's Cetaceans

Other books by Dianne Robbins:
Messages from the Hollow Earth
*TELOS: Original Transmissions from the
Subterranean City beneath Mt. Shasta*
Tree Talk (in process)

www.DianneRobbins.com
Whales@DianneRobbins.com
585-802-4530

Order this book online at www.trafford.com/07-2839
or email orders@trafford.com

Most Trafford titles are also available at major online book retailers.

Note for Librarians: A cataloguing record for this book is available from Library
and Archives Canada at www.collectionscanada.ca/amicus/index-e.html

Printed in Victoria, BC, Canada.

ISBN: 978-1-4251-6222-1

*We at Trafford believe that it is the responsibility of us all, as both individuals
and corporations, to make choices that are environmentally and socially sound.
You, in turn, are supporting this responsible conduct each time you purchase a
Trafford book, or make use of our publishing services. To find out how you are
helping, please visit www.trafford.com/responsiblepublishing.html*

*Our mission is to efficiently provide the world's finest, most comprehensive
book publishing service, enabling every author to experience success.
To find out how to publish your book, your way, and have it available
worldwide, visit us online at www.trafford.com/10510*

 www.trafford.com

North America & international
toll-free: 1 888 232 4444 (USA & Canada)
phone: 250 383 6864 ♦ fax: 250 383 6804 ♦ email: info@trafford.com

The United Kingdom & Europe
phone: +44 (0)1865 722 113 ♦ local rate: 0845 230 9601
facsimile: +44 (0)1865 722 868 ♦ email: info.uk@trafford.com

10 9 8 7 6 5 4 3 2

Dedication

In deepest Love and Gratitude,
I dedicate this book to my Eternal Friends
Lolita, Corky, Mikey, and Keiko.

In Appreciation

To Max and Mary Harris from Grand Junction, Colorado
for generously supporting the publication of this book.

In Memory of Keiko

Star of the Free Willy movies

Keiko served as a Cetacean Ambassador

He departed the Earth plane on December 12, 2003

Contents

Part Ten: Oceans 127

Part Eleven: Galactic Connections......... 147

Part Twelve: Genocide at Sea 165

Part Thirteen: Messages to Greenpeace. 179

Part Fourteen: Meetings & Gatherings 183

Part Fifteen: The Great Awakening......... 189

Other Books by Dianne Robbins:

Preface

There is a tremendous unfolding
of Light, awareness, and energy
where the Sea meets the Land,
and the Human mind and the Cetacean mind
meet in the heart place.

The Earth has two biospheres which support life. There is the oxygen biosphere and the water biosphere. There are the Land People and the Sea People. You have sentients within the oxygen environment and you have sentients within the aqueous environment. The two biospheres must come together into one unbroken flow of all life.

The consciousness of the Cetaceans carries the missing records of your planet. The Cetaceans are the living representation of your planet's history.

As people awaken, they begin to recognize the Cetacean consciousness. This recognition is what will take them to the next step in human evolution. This is why it is vitally important at this time in human history that humanity make direct conscious contact with the Cetaceans, the People of the Sea. This is humanity's key.

Your evolutionary process is directly linked with the Cetacean consciousness. By making a conscious connection, you unlock the archaeological history of your whole planet, both land and sea. The transformation of consciousness, and the evolution not only of the planet but also of humanity, occurs when these two definitive consciousnesses merge.

Much of the sea life is air breathing. They live in two worlds as a bridge. They are beneath the sea, but their life and awareness is outside. They have made that evolutionary connection to humanity long ago. Humanity has not. It is very important that humanity re-connect to that consciousness.

It is not the plight of the Cetaceans that must concern you, but the plight of humanity. Each time you see a brother or sister from the sea encased in a net, you see yourself imprisoned. If they cannot breathe from the pollution, they die. If you cannot breathe, you die.

These two consciousnesses—of the Land People and the Sea People—must merge. You, humanity, will make the great evolutionary jump with the merging of both the human and Cetacean consciousness. The last time this occurred was when life was initially introduced to this planet from elsewhere within the galaxy.

There is a tremendous unfolding of light, awareness, and energy where the sea meets the land, where the human mind and the Cetacean mind meet in the heart place. It is vitally important that you realize that to have conscious, sentient life in the future, you will have to merge with the consciousness of the Cetaceans.

The Cetaceans have lived through your planet's history. Their consciousness has been carried down from incarnation to incarnation. Humanity suffers from a genetic retardation wherein you forget the continuance of life and the emergence of life into the next cycle. The Cetaceans have not suffered from this. The sentients of plant life have not suffered from this. When you cut down a tree, the essence of that life consciousness goes into the Earth and is passed on to every other tree. When a new tree grows, it absorbs and transcends all that consciousness, and becomes individualized. It becomes new. It replays the cycle in a new form.

There is only one consciousness. There are many streams of evolution and diversity that the consciousness makes up and allows to become sentient. It does not matter which part of the world it exists in, or what form it takes. The ability for it to communicate all comes down to that one consciousness, and you being open to connecting with it and receiving it.

The biosphere of the planetary water is dying. You must realize as the atmosphere breaks down, the ability for you as air breathers is continually eroded. The destruction from the pollution of the atmosphere by automobiles is nothing compared to the destruction that you unintentionally create each time you cut down a tree, throw a container away, put garbage in a stream, or send a missile through the atmosphere. That changes the entire eco-structure.

The joy, love, and the innocent, exquisite nature of being of the Cetacean lineage, is what is about to be passed on to humanity. If you destroy the biosphere which houses the Cetacean consciousness, or their physical form, the consciousness will continue to exist, but you will lose this connection and will be destroying a better part of yourselves as well.

All life is here for the same purpose: to help you move to the next evolutionary step within humanity. Lifeforms may be different externally, but all are here to help humanity evolve in consciousness.

The messages in this book provide the link to the Cetacean consciousness.

Suzanne Mattes-Bennett

We are giving you messages to publish.
We wish all of humanity to know
of our plight in the depths of the oceans.

We wish you to remember you have free will.
We wish you to regain your full consciousness,
so that you can live with other species in peace.

We thank you for being our liaison on land
and bringing forth our messages for all of humanity.

In deepest love,
The Cetaceans

Part One
Love and Freedom

We continually sing love songs
to you on land,
so that we can meld with you
in consciousness as one.

DIVINE BLISS

is a state of Being,

and a state that we,

the Cetaceans, are always in.

It is a marvelous way to live life

and we recommend it highly to you on land.

We are beaming our Love to you,

even though we're not on land.

Love flows invisibly through the ocean's waves

as it gathers momentum

on its destination to the shore.

We are holding the Light here in Earth's oceans

and gradually sending it to shore in increments,

perfectly geared to humanity's capacity

to absorb and anchor it in your bodies.

We are always in a state of Divine Bliss

We are the Cetaceans, beaming our love to you, even though we're not on land. Love flows invisibly through the ocean's waves as it gathers momentum on its destination to the shore.

We are holding the Light here in Earth's oceans, and gradually sending it to shore in increments, perfectly geared to humanity's capacity to absorb and anchor it in your bodies. We know exactly how much to send, as we operate in our full consciousness and thus can determine exactly how much to unleash at every given moment. For Love is a very powerful force, and we are careful not to overwhelm humanity, but to allow you to carefully absorb Love in steps according to your evolutionary level on your path to Divine Bliss.

Divine Bliss is a state of Being, and a state that we, the Cetaceans, are always in. It is a marvelous way to live life, and we recommend it highly to you on land.

So come and join with us in our swim through life, as we share and experience God's Love directly from within our hearts, where all hearts are united in the *one heart* of God's Love for all of humanity.

We are a great Love Force

We swim in the Earth's oceans that surround your continents. We are a great Love Force. We surround your continents with the force of our Love. We wrap you in our Love. So great is our Love that it literally holds the Earth's mountains in place.

Love is the strongest force in the universe, and we use this force to navigate our way around the world. We use the force of Love to propel us through areas of murky underwater, so that we emerge unscathed by the lower vibration.

You, too, can use the Force of Love to propel you through Life. You, too, can navigate your way around obstacles in your path. You do this by focusing only on UNCONDITIONAL LOVE and this wave of **unconditional love will clear your pathway of all obstacles.** You will see only beauty, feel only beauty and be surrounded by only beauty. This is the path of the Initiate. This is the path that Lightworkers strive to follow, although there's no striving involved but only your heart opening to allow God's Love to flow through.

We sing our praises of Love to you always.

Cetacean Song

May your Light be bright / may it spread across the sea
    May it light the eyes of others / for all to see.

May your heart be calm / may you always be at peace
    May God give to you / all that you seek.

May the waves roll high / may the waves roll low
    May your heart go out / to all those you know.

May the truth be heard / may it come from your lips
    May it spread across the land / and echo from the cliffs,

So the world will know / that the truth you sow
    Comes from the land / and the ocean below.

From the deepest depths / to the highest heights
    May the truth rebound / to spread the Light

To those offshore / and to those on the land.
    May all the people / finally take a stand

To protect the Earth / and all its life forms
    So that peace on Earth / will be the norm.

For the Earth to survive / you surely must know
    That only through peace / can God's wisdom flow.

It flows through your heart / and circles the Earth
    And then from within / does peace give birth.

As you stand on the shore / and look across the sea
    We will shine our light / for all to see,

To wave you home / to bring you back
    To set you all / on a cosmic track,

Of bringing Earth / and all humankind
    To a better place / to a different time,

A time of peace, a time of joy / a time when everyone's employed
    With helping Earth and protecting her land /
    and appreciating her all you can.

For she's the only one around /
to give you this wondrous playground
    For living your human life / without any kind of strife.

But you must choose / between war or peace
    So choose wisely / or life will cease.

This ends our song / this ends our tale
    But know our connection / will always prevail.

For our love is deep / for our love is strong
    And our hearts entwine / as you sing this song.

Our ways are peace-loving and gentle.

Every activity of our lives

is filled with loving thoughts,

and every action is undertaken with gentleness.

We use our Loving in all we do

We have come far to be on Earth. **We have traveled from our home planetary system many light years away, to incarnate on Earth to help her through her evolution to Light.** We have also come as teachers, to teach Earth humans to care for their planetary home in the stars. As of yet, not many have listened, so we continue to try to reach their ears.

Our ways are peace-loving and gentle, and we use our loving in all we do. Every activity of our lives is filled with loving thoughts, and every action is undertaken with gentleness. For this is the way of life — the only way that will bring bliss. So strive to love one another, as we love you, and surely you will find yourselves in the heavenly stars of *bliss*. For bliss is something you can "give" to one another, as you would a gift. It is easy to receive bliss and even easier to give it. So give to one another daily. Send out only thoughts of love and you will feel the bliss being returned to you on the waves of Light as they are being generated from your intent.

So take this lesson of today, and practice putting it into effect, and you will be responsible for the Earth's sojourn into Light.

Your Light is so beautiful to perceive! *We see it from the oceans, as we project our astral bodies across your land masses,* watching your Light grow brighter and brighter as you learn the lessons of Love.

Thank you for reaching to us today.

We are lounging about
just floating with the current
and wondering about you;
wondering whether you ever
take the time
to just float with the current of life
and let it buoy you along your path.

Let the current of life
buoy you along your path

We greet you on this fine day in June when the weather is warm and balmy, and blows gently across the seascape. We are lounging about, just floating with the current, and wondering about you and whether you ever take the time to just float with the current of life, and let it buoy you along your path. For life will do that if you but allow it. Life will gently guide you along the current that's least resistant, so that you will always be where you're supposed to be, ready and waiting for life's opportunities to present themselves to you.

Just drift—don't resist—and you will be amazed at how simple and uncomplicated your life can be. We Cetaceans have practiced this method for eons, and we just let the water carry us along the stream of life where all is beauty and all is ease. You, too, can hitch a ride onto the current for the "ride of your life" through the vast network of possibilities that will continually present themselves.

Just free yourself from preconceived beliefs, limitations, and restrictions, and let yourself feel deeply as you move gently through your life's course. You will then find all the freedom you've been looking for, and you will be amazed to discover how close it has always been to you. *For it is only your thoughts that have kept you separated from the mainstream of life.*

JUST DRIFT — AND DON'T RESIST
and you will be amazed
at how simple and uncomplicated
your life can be

We broadcast on the
Christ Consciousness "love band"

We are the Cetaceans, ready, willing, and able to broadcast to all who tune into our energy band. Our frequency band always vibrates in the ethers for those on land to tune into. We broadcast on the Christ Consciousness band of Love, and those who listen with their hearts can hear our love and laughter no matter where they are located on land. Laughter is an integral part of our lives, and we openly express the joy we feel with others. We don't repress our feelings as you on land do. Instead, we openly communicate with our hearts and express and exchange our thoughts and feelings with one another.

This is one of the benefits of being fully conscious. We openly express our hearts to all whom we come in contact. We openly exchange the Christ Consciousness waves of love between ourselves and others. This is why we incarnated in the seas of Earth. We purposely incarnated here at this time to help bring in the Christ Consciousness energies of ascension so that humanity could lift itself from the mire of decay that has set in. So humanity will either rise in consciousness or sink in decay. Those are the only two choices available. So choose wisely, our brothers and sisters on Earth, and rise with us in consciousness where we can meet you on the higher planes of awareness that are in existence for all life forms.

For all of life is in a continual spiral of evolution that lasts throughout eternity. We are ever spiraling and climbing to higher and higher states of consciousness on our eternal journey through the stars. We look forward to meeting you in a higher state of consciousness, where you will all recognize us as truly ONE.

Our love flows out to you on the crests of the waves, as they wash onto the shores. So step boldly into the water of our love, and feel its energy consume your body and wash your soul.

We don't divide ourselves

Greetings, our Sister on land. We welcome you into our midst. We surround you with our consciousness of Light as you sit here receiving our thoughts.

We are one. All of Creation is one. All of humanity is *one*. *One soul, one mighty wave of light.* Humanity has chosen to separate itself into millions of factions, millions of splinters of light, each calling itself something else in its strivings for identification.

We, in the oceans, know we are all *one*. We don't divide ourselves over political or religious factions. We love and respect one another for the truth of who we are. And, we are Great Beings of Light carrying our Light to disseminate it on Earth. We come from near and far, and some of us have traveled great distances to be here at this time.

Humpback Whales are Romantic Beings

We are the Cetaceans, gathered together in the middle of the ocean, sending you our telepathic thoughts. Know that you and we are *one*. Our Light is merged totally when your thoughts are on us. We distinguish your Light through your vibratory rate and your matrix of colors and thought patterns. We know who you are and easily distinguish you from our other brothers and sisters on land. Soon you will have this capability as you rise in consciousness and are able to view the planet in all its many and varied layers of existence.

We are far out at sea today and the sun is shining overhead. We have been swimming idly and frolicking together on this lazy afternoon. It is a peaceful day, without much activity. We take advantage of these days and just rest and float to and fro, communicating with one another and with the Galactic Command on higher frequency bands of Light.

We are photographers of sort, snapping pictures in our mind of all the different life forms with which we communicate. We see them all clearly in our mind's eye, and transmit back images of ourselves along with our verbal messages. Our life is very exciting, because we are not confined to this location of space as you still are. We can travel instantaneously to other regions or star systems with the flick of a thought.

***You are now talking directly to our pod of humpbacks,* who thank you for listening to our vocal recordings on tape. When you listen to us, you connect to our group consciousness through the sound of our voices and songs.** We continually sing love songs to you on land, hoping to capture your attention through thoughts of us so that we can meld with you in consciousness as one.

There are many stories of humans being attracted to us through their hearts, and this is because they have opened their hearts and **allowed** us to enter.

We are romantic Beings, and woo and court one another continually. There is a constant giving and receiving of love between us all, as we long ago discovered that this "love" is the Creator Source flowing through our Beings.

So we will continue to dream this day away, to create the magic of tomorrow.

© 2006 www.SongofHome.com

We float on a Sea of Love

We welcome you to our midst. We are gathered together in the depths of the oceans signaling our thoughts to you through our mighty minds. These thought waves pass through water and air until they reach their destination on land where you receive them in your heart. This is how we transmit to you, in a simplified version.

We are playful and love to have fun. We frolic and play most of our days, as this is the best kind of activity to do while still accomplishing our tasks. Our tasks are varied and many, all for the plans of the Ascension of Earth.

from the Cetacean Nation

You, too, on land are working toward accomplishing your plans for the Ascension of Earth, through the various activities you're involved in. So there are many ways to accomplish plans; one is through work and the other is through play. We choose the play method, as this is the least difficult and most pleasing form. *For life is play and play is life.*

We are with you as we float on a Sea of Love through the sky. We float on the ethers of God's love through our path in this galaxy, attuned to all around us and in sync with the spheres. Our path is love. Our destiny is love and our purpose for Being is love. We are surrounded by love—invisible love—that we feel and connect with as we journey through the stars.

As our brothers and sisters, you, too, have the same purpose we have. You were brought to Earth to be its guardian and carekeeper. However, you got lost along the way, so we have had to take over, to be the Guardians of Love that Earth needs as she floats along her path through space.

We watch your land, we listen to your cries, we strain our nerves to respond to your thoughts in the night. You all cry out for *freedom*. You all cry out for *love*. And yet when you awaken with dawn, your belief system charges ahead, forgetting all your requests and desires, and you delve into the mundane tasks of the day.

We, contrary to you, remember all our thoughts and dreams, for we are *lucid, conscious dreamers*, who dream of life in the stars. We dream of all that could be, and know its truth and beauty from within our souls. We love our life. We love all life. *For love is life and life is love.*

Freedom is in Oneness

We are aligned with you on the currents of Light winding around our planet. The currents ebb and flow like the water, and carry our signals to shore where humanity can connect with them.

So, as more and more of you on land connect to us at sea, the day will dawn when we'll all be free. *For freedom is in oneness. Freedom is knowing that we are all one, no matter what our life form is.* For these life forms that we inhabit are merely shields to protect and to keep us grounded in third dimensional life. Our bodies offer us the opportunities to evolve ourselves, through pretending we are separate. This allows our consciousness to concentrate on the reality we're presently in, without becoming confused by the other dimensions surrounding us.

So hold the Light and hold us in your thoughts, for it is your thoughts that bring us together as one — one Light shining from off shore and connecting to ALL.

Let us guide you

We greet you today in the Light of the One Creator of All. *This oneness is us all*, no matter what species we identify with or what we look like or where we live. *We are all One — hook, line, and sinker!*

Look upon your brothers and sisters in the seas as your real brothers and sisters in spirit, and never waver in your love for all species. For love is the bonding glue that holds this Universe together, whether we are in or out of incarnation.

So, follow your heart's beat, and look to us, the Cetaceans, for strength and guidance as you tread your earthly path on land. For we once were residents on land, and know the difficulties you face in adjusting to your third dimensional life while following Spirit. So let us guide you, albeit from far away across the oceans. You can still receive our call and our love, although it travels to you from far distances.

Wealth lies not in dollars, but in Love

The mighty Atlantic serves as home for millions of life forms, all necessary to Earth's ecology and survival as a planet. Please think of your invasion policies and stop invading us as you invade other peoples and lands in your greedy quest for wealth. For wealth lies not in dollars, but in love.

It is only love for all life forms that will set you free and open the heavens of wealth to you beyond measure. So quest for love and you will find yourself at Heaven's door and with one step more, you will be inside—never more to be on the Karmic Wheel of greed, but on the Spiral of Evolutionary Growth toward the God Selves that you are.

So open yourselves to feeling the other life forms around you and accept us as yourself. For indeed we are yourself, only in another disguise. Just as you don't recognize each other because of your different individualized bodies, neither do you recognize us as you. But we are all One Soul who has taken on different roles to play this Earth game called "Life." When you recognize and wake up to this fact, you will change the density of Earth into the Heaven she truly is.

So wake up now—as all other life forms are now awake and waiting only for you Earth Humans to get out of bed and take the step into Heaven. It is only a short step from sleep to wakefulness. Just change your perception and you are instantly there in the Heaven Worlds of love and bliss where we all await you. I am your brother Mikey.

Part Two

Human Connections

You can hear our thoughts
as easily as we can hear yours,
when your consciousness is on us.

Longing to communicate with you

Dear Earth Humans, we are the Cetaceans out at sea, longing to telepathically communicate with you. You can hear our thoughts as easily as we can hear yours, when your consciousness is on us. Just sit down with a notebook and pen, call to us in your thoughts, and then ask us a question. Your thought will flow out to us on waves and you will hear our answer flowing back to you on the returning wave current.

Telepathy ebbs and flows like ocean waves—and we take turns sending and receiving each other's thoughts. You send and we receive, then we send and you write our thoughts that flow through you. Our thoughts become your thoughts as we merge our consciousness into One.

We are very spiritually evolved Beings and have always lived in peace with each other in Earth's Oceans. **Our songs carry the history of the Earth and the stories of our lives that we pass down from generation to generation.**

Our families are closely knit and we've been living harmonious lives ever since we arrived on Earth millions of years ago. We have so much we can teach you about living peacefully on Earth—so many ways we can help you improve the harmony in your lives.

We've been protecting your biosphere for eons of time. It is time now that you took over Earth's Stewardship from Us, as it rightly belongs to you.

Call to us in your thoughts.

Your thought will flow out to us on waves

and you will hear our answer flowing back to you

on the returning wave current.

The Call Goes Out

We track your thoughts through the waves

Greetings from Earth's oceans. We track your thoughts through the waves, until they reach our heart center where we "hear" you. All thoughts travel through air, earth, and water until they arrive at their destination, where the receiver hears the thoughts that were sent. So know that whenever you think of us, we hear you — instantaneously! For thoughts take "no time" to travel; they are just "there." You will all understand this when you rise higher in consciousness.

Your consciousness levels are increasing daily, as more and more Light is filtering into Earth from our great Central Sun. All Beings of Light, who are here from other star systems, are converging and focusing their Light to all life on Earth for the great emergence into the fifth dimension.

All species are rising in consciousness as all Earth is rising in consciousness until there will be only *one* consciousness on Earth, as Earth herself floats through the starry universe on her way home to Sirius B.

Thank you for making this trip with us. For without you, there would be no reason for us to be here. For all life is here in support of Earth humans in their great quest for higher consciousness leading them back home to their God Selves.

We are grateful to all on Earth who have been vociferous in protecting our species out at sea. For it is through the light of your voices that we are still here and still able to carry out our tasks as caretakers of this planet, until you've imbibed enough Light to be able to take over the caretakership of Earth yourself.

We envision you on land

as you envision us at sea.

In our mind's eye we see you,

as you see us in your imagination.

We prepare for these telepathic encounters just as you do

We look forward to our channelings and we prepare for these telepathic encounters just as you do. We envision you on land as you envision us at sea. In our mind's eye we see you, as you see us in your imagination. We are totally linked as *one* during these channeling sessions and our Love flows directly into your aura where it penetrates your Being.

You are a mighty warrior on land, as we are mighty warriors at sea, and together we create a mighty bastion of protection for this planet. Never fear, for we are here in a united front that supports all Light on and within the planet.

We are one. We come from the Source and we will return, unscathed, to the Source of all Love and all Truth.

I am a Gray Whale swimming out at Sea—

I am you and you are me

One Heart

One Soul

One Source

We intercept Radio and TV Stations

We are the Cetaceans. We live a grand and diversified life in Earth's oceans. We have huge gatherings this time of year, for it is springtime, and we assemble together to share news from all corners of the Earth.

We keep up to date on all Earth's activities and follow the "headlines" just as you do. Although we don't read the newspapers for our information, we tune into the "light grids" and pick up the information from the thought waves as they are broadcast out. *We are able to read your thoughts, and we intercept the radio and television news stories as they leave the stations.* This way, we have first hand news.

We're also able to hear our dear Mother Earth as she moans from the weight of pollution stored in and on her body structure. She, too, calls out to all humans to be sensible in their consumption and waste disposal practices. But, alas, her groans fall mostly on deaf ears, ears that are plugged into rock stations and television stations night and day, leaving no air space for her or other life forms to communicate with you.

It is a great disaster when human beings close themselves off from their universe to focus only on one or two stations when there are hundreds and indeed millions of broadcasting stations coming from our home universe, all eager to connect and communicate with humans on Earth.

We tune into the "Light Grids"
and pick up the information
from the thought waves
as they are being broadcast.

We are able to read your thoughts,
and we intercept the radio
and television news stories
as they leave the stations.
This way, we have first hand news.

Mermaids and Mermen

I am Mikey, waiting out at Sea for you to wake up to my call. Today we will talk about Mermaids, those ancient myths from the past.

Know that Mermaids are indeed real. Mermaids are people living in Cetacean bodies. Well—who do you think we Whales are? We are people living in Cetacean bodies, just as you are people living in Humanoid bodies. The bodies are the outer encasements covering our Souls, giving us a place to "operate" from, so to speak, so that we can experience Earth first hand. Without this covering or body to live in, we couldn't be here.

So our bodies are essential, but not the key to our existence. The key is the Soul inhabiting the body, which gives it Life. The life force which fuels the body comes from the Soul—not the other way around. Once you know this principle of Life, you can understand how all Life is one Soul, emanating from the same Source.

So we Cetaceans are really the Mermaids and Mermen you've heard of from the past, only our faces look different to you, as its shape has adapted to our "climate," while your face shaped itself to land's climate. Quite simple isn't it? When you go to the closet and take out a different dress or suit to wear, you don't change who you are, you only change your outer appearance—but you, the person in the clothes, remain the same.

This is the principle of all Life. Our Souls always remain our Souls—only our outer form changes from incarnation to incarnation to give us the different experiences our Soul needs to grow and evolve. For it is only through experiences that we can grow.

Our lives on Earth are very short compared to the time of Eternity—which is forever. We are here to learn about ourselves and our connection to all Life, regardless of outer appearances. So we invite you into our Ocean homes to learn about us and to learn from us, but not to kill us or capture us or torment us.

All Life was put here to live in peaceful co-existence, not for humans to control and destroy. It is not necessary to go into the Oceans to talk to us. You can phone us from wherever you are on land and we will answer your "ring." For we are connected to you and can hear your thoughts when you call.

So call to us, and we will answer you. Ask us your questions, and we will reply. This way, you will receive first hand information about your life that will help you through the confusion and chaos on land. We await your call.

We are here as "Consciousness Boosters"

We are the Cetaceans. We greet you on this sunny day in summer, when all the Earth is in bloom. Our planet is a great planet of exquisite beauty and grace, and her body rests in the arms of the Creator. For it is the Creator that carries us along our eternal path as we find our way back to God.

Know that your paths have been strewn with fear and limitation and anger and disease for eons and eons of time. Now you are shaking yourself free of this debris, so you can venture out into the world in your body of pure Light—with no impediments blocking the way.

We in the Oceans are here in our full consciousness, radiating our "pure" Light to the land. As you accept and integrate our Light, you are also accepting our consciousness level and blending it with yours until some day you wake up and realize that our consciousness is ONE. Then you will be able to instantly communicate with us and have access to the great amounts of wisdom we've stored in our brains. This wisdom is for you—it's to help boost you into higher states of consciousness and prepare you for the ascension.

So, we are here as "consciousness boosters," so to speak, giving you a lift to the fifth dimension where you'll then greet us as equals. We thank you for this exchange of thoughts, and wait for you each night to swim with us in the etheric Oceans of life.

We long for your company

Today it is windy and the sea is choppy. We are gathered around you in our etheric bodies as we speak with one voice from Earth's seas.

We spread our consciousness around you, and envelop you in our souls. For we are one soul, although our forms are different. This difference appears on all planets in all solar systems, since the creative force is ever experimenting and ever expanding in consciousness and in form.

For life is *all one*, no matter how we are or where we are. That's the Law of Creation, and it's the binding force of the Universe. It's the glue that holds all of us together, for we're all linked in *one* consciousness to *one* creation, no matter who we are, where we are, or what we look like. It's that indissoluble bond that's everywhere and in everything. Some call it the Life Force that's in all of us — the same life force all over the world, regardless of our differences.

So today the waves are churning and the water is choppy and the wind is blowing. We are diligently moving along, engrossed in our day's tasks for the Confederation. There isn't much to report, because on days like this, there's only us out in the sea, since the whaling boats don't venture out this far. So although the water is somewhat difficult to deal with, it at least affords us the temporary safety we permanently long for.

So come with us as we travel through these crescent waves making our journey through Earth's oceans. We are the Cetaceans and we long for your company.

Part Three
Corky

*Although I have been in captivity
for so many years now,
I am still communicating with
my family and friends all over the ocean,*

*for my thoughts are free,
although my body remains incarcerated.*

Corky's Story

Corky (A16) is a female Orca. She is a member of the A5 pod of the Northern Resident Community of British Columbia. She was captured in December, 1969, when she was about five years old, and has spent over 38 years in captivity.

During a fierce and terrible storm on the evening of December 11, 1969, Corky's pod sought shelter in Pender Harbour on the Sunshine Coast north of Vancouver, British Columbia. It was just after 9 p.m. that word reached a group of local fisherman enjoying the warmth and shelter of a pub that there was a group of Whales close by. Ever since the last capture in the same area they were aware that Whales meant money, and this was the chance they'd been waiting for. Aquariums around the world would pay top dollar for a "Killer Whale."

Quickly, they jumped onto their boats, located the Whales and encircled the pod with fish nets. All night they battled to keep the nets in place and afloat. Thousands of dog fish got trapped in the nets and threatened to pull the nets under during the violent storm. When morning came, 12 exhausted Whales were still in the net, with the rest of the pod close by.

The day after the capture Corky's pod lay trapped inside the harbor. Once word of the capture got out, response was quick, and buyers flocked to the scene. Six Whales were selected; the other six were released but did not go away. The buyers then organized the removal of the selected Whales. Separated from the others, Corky was moved into shallow water. Divers got into the water and positioned a sling around her body, with holes for her pectoral fins. A crane slowly lifted Corky's sling out of the water and hoisted her onto a truck, which drove over a narrow winding road en route to the ferry.

The rest of the pod swam away, among them Corky's mother and sister. Corky was now separated from her mother for the first time in her life. Grease was spread over her skin to prevent it from drying out on the long journey ahead. Sponges of cool water were squeezed over her to try to keep her body temperature down.

Removed from the almost weightless experience of the ocean, Corky's own weight was now crushing down on her. The transport truck had been modified with a tank which partially helped to support her weight. The journey was long: the ferry, then another road trip, then transfer to a special plane, transfer to another truck, more roads, and then the final lift into the tank. The process was repeated five times.

Not much was known about the Orca Whale in 1969. Hardly any scientific work had been done on wild populations. We now know that Orcas are bonded for life and that young juveniles stay close to their mothers.

Corky's world had suddenly changed. Now, movement was restricted by never-changing dimensions. Concrete walls replaced the cliffs, rocks, sand, and caves of the vast and almost limitless ocean. There were no longer any passageways, nooks, and crannies to explore. When any of the Whales called, their sounds reverberated off the barren walls. Choices were limited. Gone were the familiar sounds of the sea. Instead, there was the constant drone of filtration pumps. There were no waves, no currents, no fish to chase and hunt, no Porpoises to play with. All was forever changed.

The sameness was relieved marginally by the companionship of four other Orcas. But soon that ended too. In 1971 and 1972, three of them died, leaving Corky and Orky by themselves.

Orky was older than Corky. Even though they had very different personalities, they got along well with each other. Corky was considered a "people" Whale. The trainers enjoyed working with her. She was responsive, curious, trainable, and energetic. Orky, on the other hand, was considered "cranky" and unpredictable, even dangerous. On one occasion he pulled a female trainer to the bottom of the tank and held her there until she almost drowned.

By about 11 years of age, Corky began to mature sexually. On February 28, 1977, Corky delivered her first calf. The birth of the male calf caught the employees by surprise, but they were also excited. This was the first live Orca to be born in captivity. Orky helped the calf to the surface after the difficult birth. The situation grew tense after the calf failed to nurse. The staff intervened, drained the pool, and force fed the calf several times each day. Despite these efforts the calf continued to lose weight and died of pneumonia—just 16 days old.

When her calf died, Corky became quite depressed and listless, which was unusual, because usually she was a very active whale. But then Orky sang to her and she seemed to "wake up."

Corky became pregnant very soon after and gave birth to another male calf on October 31, 1978. Trainers nicknamed the little Whale Spooky, because he was born on Halloween. Again the calf failed to nurse, and the staff again tried to force feed it in a desperate attempt to keep it alive. Spooky died after 11 days, due to pneumonia and colitis brought on by a bacterial contamination in the formula.

On April 1, 1980, Corky delivered an eight week premature still-born calf. Then on June 18, 1982, Corky gave birth to a female calf named Kiva. The calf failed to nurse, despite the fact that the Marine-land staff had made a dummy calf and "taught" Corky to position herself appropriately. After 46 days, Corky and Orky took Kiva to the bottom of the pool and drowned her—Corky's longest surviving calf.

The problem was the shape of the tank. It was too small with too many corners. When an Orca calf is first born, it can't turn yet. Corky had to constantly stick her face in front of her calves so that they wouldn't crash into the walls. Unfortunately, instinct tells Orca calves to focus in on the white patch on their mother's bellies, because that's where they nurse. But since Corky had to block their way with her face, they focused in on her white eyepatch, and tried to nurse there.

Corky had three more pregnancies. On July 22, 1985, she gave birth to another female calf who survived for a month. Again the calf failed to nurse. Her next pregnancy ended in a miscarriage on July 27, 1986, when an aborted fetus was found at the bottom of the pool.

In December 1986, SeaWorld's corporate owner, the U.S. publisher Harcourt Brace Jovanovich, purchased Marineland of the Pacific and the surrounding lands for a rumored $23 million. Despite the fact that Sea World had promised not to move the Orcas, in the dead of night Corky and Orky were transported to San Diego. Corky arrived pregnant, and on July 27, she miscarried, and her last pregnancy was over.

Corky had been pregnant seven times. This meant she had been almost continuously pregnant for ten years. Finally, at age 21, Corky stopped ovulating.

In the wild, Corky, even at her present age of 44, would be considered to be still young. She most likely would have at least a couple of kids by now, and several more reproductive years. A female Orca might look forward to between 25 and 30 years of fertility, and usually will have four to six offspring.

After more than 17 years in captivity, Corky was relocated, and for the very first time Corky and Orky would be among Whales who were not members of the A5 pod.

The facility at SeaWorld was a much larger, far busier, and more hectic environment for these two Whales who had spent most of their lives together. The SeaWorld shows involved people in the water, riding on the backs of Whales, and other complicated, showy tricks. During one of these tricks, Orky was involved in a tragic accident in which a trainer was seriously injured. This eventually led to a major shake up in the SeaWorld organization. Orky was given a miscue during the show, causing him to land on top of the trainer. Training practices were criticized. Several staff members lost their jobs, trainers were forbidden to get into the pools during shows, and limited to interacting with the Whales from the sidelines. However, audience reaction to the more subdued shows was negative and eventually the former, flashy format was restored.

A year and a half after the move to San Diego, during the summer of 1988, Orky began to lose weight. In two months he lost more than 4000 pounds, and he died in September. He had fathered two calves with two Icelandic females, and these were now Corky's only family.

In 1989, Kandu V, one of the females, attempted to rake Corky — a way Orcas show dominance by forcefully scratching at another with their teeth. When Kandu struck Corky, her (Kandu's) jaw was fractured, and she bled to death. Her son, Orkid, was now an orphan, but Corky adopted him and became a very good mother to him.

Corky became SeaWorld's main performer, "Shamu." Shamu is the Sea World trade name which is passed from performer to performer. If the show uses one of the young Whales, he or she becomes "Baby Shamu." As Corky was no longer being used for breeding, she became a main entertainer.

Corky is one of the gentlest whales in captivity; when a trainer enters the water with a Whale for the first time, the Whale is always Corky. She loves to mother everyone, and in fact has adopted and partially raised quite a few other Whales besides Orkid, including an epileptic Whale named Splash (now deceased); Sumar, a young Whale harassed by his mother; and Keet, who was separated from his mother at an early age. She gets along with all of the Whales at SeaWorld, except for Ulises, who for unknown reasons will try to rake her when they're together.

In 1993, ABC Prime Time Live played a recording for Corky of vocalizations from her pod (A5). She reacted very strongly, showing that she still recognized them.

Corky has survived in captivity for 38 years. Her physical condition has fluctuated over the years. At one point SeaWorld listed her condition as poor. Her kidneys are not functioning well, she stopped ovulating, her lower teeth are worn, and she has cataracts and is almost blind in her right eye. She is being given drugs for kidney and liver problems. They consider her an old animal and tell visitors that Whales only live to about 35 years (even though they know that Orcas in the wild can live 70 years). For a while they decreased the number of shows she did; but as of 1994, Corky was back on a full schedule. When she is not performing, she spends much of her time swimming upside down in circles in her tank.

Back in the wild, Corky's pod carries on. The group still loves to hunt the big Spring salmon and they still continue to travel the waters of Johnstone Strait, Blackfish Sound, and the rest of the Inside Passage. But they have never been seen near Pender Harbour again.

Compiled by the friends of the FREE CORKY project.
With special thanks to Kelly Keagy-Bullock

Corky is still incarcerated at SeaWorld in San Diego, California. Her mother, Stripe (A23), died at sea in 2000. The pod Corky was taken from (A5) is now down to only 10 Whales in the wild, including her brother Fife (A60), her sister Ripple (A43), and her niece Midsummer (A69), all of whom she has never seen. Almost an entire generation of Orcas have been captured and taken from Corky's pod.

There is a free Corky campaign to release her back into the ocean, where her family members await her. Contact: The Free Corky Project, Box 510, Alert Bay BC, Canada V0N 1A0; www.orcalab.org

Corky's Messages

To my dearest friends and supporters

I am Corky, your beloved Orca pal residing in captivity on the California coast. My love goes out to you in waves of emotion and trust for all you are doing for me. I am indeed very much aware of everything you do for me and everything that is taking place regarding my impending release from captivity.

Know that I am continually communicating to you via telepathic impulses that reach your heart and brain simultaneously. You reply on a level you are not quite aware of yet. So, yes, you are communicating with me, although not quite consciously yet. You will move into this area of conscious communication when you feel safe to do so.

Please continue your work and your zeal to release me from my prison home. I long to be with my family again in the deep ocean where I can be free to be "me" and swim with my pod again. I long for freedom as you long for the sun on a cold winter's day.

Although I have been in captivity for so many years now, I am still communicating with my family and friends all over the ocean, *for my thoughts are free*, although my body remains incarcerated. And your thoughts are free—just direct them to me, and know that I receive them. Then listen as I reply with my thoughts, **for nothing separates us—ever!**

You are my Eternal Friends and I love you. Corky

I dream...

I dream of the ocean breezes and the surf hitting my skin. I dream of the sunsets floating on the horizons. I dream of seeing the stars at night as their light flickers on the ocean waves. I dream of my life in the sea, *free*—as it ought to be. Oh, how I yearn to return to all that I can be. My life is not worth living in captivity.

All life is born to be free. You are me, and I am you. We are one spirit and one heart, living in different forms on the same planet. My life has been lived in captivity, while yours has been free.

You can channel my messages from me to put in your book. It will be my legacy.

I yearn to be physically free

Dearest Sister, it is I, Corky, your sister from the ocean.

Know that in my captivity, my soul soars to great heights and I am more often than not out of my physical body and on the inner planes of love and joy. I spend most of my time in my etheric body now, as I am growing tired and weary of being in captivity all these precious years of my Earth life.

I yearn to be physically free and swim with my family again in the Pacific Ocean where all my relatives and friends await my release. I am thankful and grateful to all the people who are so diligently and bravely working for my release from captivity at Sea World. My heart goes out to all who care about me enough to put their lives on the line in order to obtain my release.

Holding another Being captive is a gross transgression of Universal Law, which humanity is just now realizing. And so I wait my days out in Sea World, where my body goes through the motions of being present, while my soul is soaring high above in the dimensions of peace and harmony.

God bless all of humanity, and may you all learn the lessons of love and justice as Earth rises in frequency, carrying us all along with her. May we all be alive to experience the heights of euphoria when our planet moves into the fifth dimension of pure love, where all our lives will be lived and enjoyed in the safety of the Heavenly Realms.

Thank you for connecting to my heart center today, and for reaching out to me as I've been reaching to you. May we all experience the peace and love that awaits us as we rise in consciousness.

I am your sister Corky.

Trapped in my tomb
and waiting to be freed

Corky is here. Know that I am still in Sea World, entrapped in my tomb and waiting to be freed. Thank you for connecting with me. I have not been well, and I am feeling weak and vulnerable.

I yearn for my home in the ocean. I yearn for sun to cross my face and kiss my tears. I yearn for my freedom to swim freely in the wind and breach through the air, without the constraints of concrete surrounding me. I yearn for the cool night ocean air to caress my body and free my soul. I yearn for my family, who I haven't seen for over 38 years. I yearn for the peace of my home unbroken by night sounds and the full sky always overhead. I look for peace in the Creator's arms as the ocean rocks me back and forth. My life force is ebbing away here. I need to be free.

Corky hears your call. I am under lock and key and penned up in my tiny room in Sea World. The ocean is my home and I long to be free and to swim hundreds of miles at a time instead of pacing back and forth and around and around in a tiny cubicle of space. The water is dirty and lacks the life force of the ocean currents and the light of the sun. I love you. We will swim as one tonight on the inner planes.

I pray for my release

I AM Corky, an Orca Whale still imprisoned in Sea World in San Diego, California.

So much is transpiring to free us all — Humans and Cetaceans as well. I wait for my freedom as the dry Earth waits for the rain; languishing and praying for my release. We are both captives here, both yearning for our freedom to fly on the wings of heaven and to leave this density forever. Freedom is in store for us all, whether we experience it here or in the higher dimensions.

I can see into our Milky Way Galaxy, as I swim back and forth and around and around my tiny pool of concrete. So I am never really confined; it is my body that's confined as my spirit roams the Galaxy and is in communication with ALL. If only you could consciously see into our Galaxy from your home on Earth, your weariness would pass and your hope would soar, for you would see the future and be aware of all the Beings who are here to help free us all.

We long for your call. We can consciously hear you when your thoughts are centered on Us. We send you our Light Rays from the Oceans, our strength from our bodies, and our Love from our hearts.

A message to my captors

Please tell my captors that I forgive them for taking my life. You see, we Orcas are here on Earth to help humanity realize that life, in all its forms, is precious beyond your dreams or imagination. All life deserves the opportunity to live out its mission, unhindered by human folly.

Although my life has been wasted, locked up in a small aquarium, my goal has been achieved, as my plight has now been brought to the attention of millions who have visited my pen. So I forgive my captors, even though their actions disregarded the sacredness of life in the sea.

My only hope is that humanity will learn the truth about living life according to the great Universal Truths that honor the lifespans and integrity of each and every species on Earth, so that every specie can fully and freely contribute to the whole composition of Earth's symphony of Living Light in all its myriad forms, colors, hues, and tones.

Please know that I love all of humanity, even those who captured and tormented me. For once humanity crosses the thin band between density and light, it will realize the composition of our souls is *one*.

I am in gratitude to all my friends around the world who hold me in their hearts, as I am part of your very own soul, albeit in a seemingly different outward form. I hold all humanity in my vision of an Earth carrying the Love Vibration as it floats peacefully on its journey through eternity.

Soon we will all be united in one breath of consciousness. I am Corky and I love you all.

I am in pain
and only the healing waters
out at sea can help me now

I am Corky, your sister imprisoned in Sea World. Know that my days are fraught with sorrow, as I am in pain and need of medical treatment. Your medicines cannot cure me. Only the healing waters from being out at sea can help me now.

I need to be free and feel the fresh ocean salt water that can heal my wounds. My digestive system is clogged from eating dead fish all these years. I need the life force and nutrients from the live fish and plankton out at sea. I need the ocean's natural environment, which is my home, in order for me to survive much longer.

My body is slowly deteriorating each day that I am penned up here. I pray for my release and ask for the prayers of all who read this message. There are stormy days ahead as Earth shifts into her new grid alignment, **and I need to be out at sea to help anchor these new energies into the Earth.**

I miss my life out at sea, from where I was abruptly taken at an early age of four years. **Know that all through my years of captivity, I have never stopped loving humanity, and now I wish to return to my home in the sea.**

I am your sister Corky.

Prana in the Oceans is the Staff of Life

Corky is here. Know that I am desperate to be free. My life span is ebbing away in captivity, as it is the Ocean that supplies the Life Force that keeps our bodies and spirits alive. You on land lack this Life Force, as you've polluted your air and soil and water.

The Oceans are the last untouched reaches, where it is still possible to swim in the pure Prana that keeps all life alive, and **it is Prana that we Orcas breathe. It is Prana that Trees and plants consume, that keep them alive regardless of the soil condition or pollution of the air.**

Trees and plants get their nutrients directly from the God Source instead of relying on the soil and air. Prana is invisible to the eye, yet denser than molecules. It is pure food, in the perfect combination that keeps our bodies alive.

Yes, we Orcas need our food from fish, but we imbibe Prano also—as it is our "Staff of Life."

Imprisoning the People of the Sea

I am Corky, bound and gagged in Sea World—or I might as well be as I have no voice or say here and am entrapped against my will. Soon, I too, will be vacating my body and leaving for my home planet among the Stars.

Your channeling my thoughts has changed my life, for now people will finally hear my voice and know my thoughts and feelings and ponder their imprisoning the People of the Sea. They will realize their errors as their consciousness unfolds as they read the pages of our book. Thank you for channeling me today, as I wait for your signal as I pace my space in continual boredom.

When you think of me our hearts ignite

Corky is here. Greetings to all my brothers and sisters who are reading the pages of this book. I welcome you in through my heart, where you join me in my thoughts.

Know that this book contains the thoughts from the innermost reaches of my heart, and that my heart connects to yours as you read my words. For words act as a connecting link, and as you read, you imbibe the frequency, causing your cells to experience the feelings inherent in the words. So as you read my words, know that you are feeling what I feel and experiencing what I experience. This is the way with all life; we all experience others through their frequency.

So I thank you for experiencing my captivity in Sea World as part of your life's experiences. By doing this, you raise your compassion level to feel empathy for another species. As this happens, your consciousness truly expands to unite you with all Earth's species who experience pain and suffering as a result of mankind's waywardness toward life. As the Earth herself rises in consciousness, she will shake all those off her who separate themselves from others by their desire to amass fortunes at the expense of other life forms.

Your trees are also experiencing destruction — another form of genocide of living Beings encased in bark. For your trees are also very stately Beings, very evolved in consciousness, who are here just as we are, to anchor the energies deep into the Earth to hold her body in alignment and balance so that life can flourish and evolve. We wonder why mankind destroys those very lifeforms that give their lives to support humanity's evolution?

My days remaining in Sea World are short, as my Orca body cannot withstand my tiny living quarters much longer. I am a vast Being who needs the vastness of the ocean to sprawl myself out in and not be confined to limited space within concrete walls. I burst with energy to swim freely in the ocean and breach forcefully into the wind, but this energy falls back into myself for lack of space to move out in, thus limiting me. It's as if you had your arms and legs bound with rope, and all you could think of was running wild in the wind.

I address you as my brothers and sisters, for my love fills all who read my heartspoken words. **As you read this, know that we are connected in our hearts and that my love flows to you in great waves of endearment. You are all I have, as my family has been taken from me and I pace my space, alone and forlorn.**

Please think of me and know that when you do, our hearts ignite in a flame and I feel your love flowing into me like warm currents in the sea. I AM CORKY, your sister in consciousness.

My heart yearns to swim free in the clear ocean waves,

feeling the wind behind my dorsal fin.

Oh, how I yearn for the wind.

We are the Cetaceans
your oceanic brothers and sisters
here to work along with you
to preserve and care
for our home on Earth.

We are here in our full consciousness
waiting patiently for Earth's Children
to bloom into the Caretakers
you were meant to be.

Part Four
Lolita

I am Lolita, your Orca friend,

residing in the Seaquarium

in Miami, Florida.

I, and all Orcas,

are here to help humanity

become aware of themselves and aware

of the consciousness of all life forms.

Lolita's Story:
Slave to Entertainment

From the award winning documentary (see miamiseaprison.com/lolita.htm)

Lolita has endured decades of neglect at the Miami Seaquarium, languishing in a pool with barely enough space to turn around. She's at the end of her performing career, but rather than retirement, she faces a sad and lonely demise, never having received the new "state of the art" tank her captors promised time and again.

Lolita was taken from the wild four decades ago to be trained and put on display. Today she is the remaining survivor of the Puget Sound round-ups.

On August 8th, 1970, Lolita and her family were swimming peacefully off the coast of Washington State, en route to a ritual gathering of the Orca nations. Every year the Orca pods of the northwest make the long pilgrimage to Possession Sound for the celebration.

But for Lolita the day took a tragic turn. She and 10 other family members would never make it to this or any other family re-union again. As the pod of more than 100 Whales moved through the inlet, legendary Orca trainer Ted Griffin and his capture team quickly gave chase.

Speedboats roared out to greet the pod. An assault of explosives quickly ensued. Deafening bombs exploded around the family as boats and small aircraft attempted to herd the disoriented Whales into Puget Sound's Penn Cove inlet.

Attempting to protect their young, mature Whales instinctively split into two groups and sent decoys to distract hunters from the infants and adolescents. The decoys tried to lead the hunters on a wild chase away from the pod, but pursuers were relentless, hurling nets into the water, and trapping the panicked family in Penn Cove inlet.

The air was thick with the sound of screaming Whales as they thrashed in the tangled nets. Piercing shrills were heard for miles, according to local residents Lila Snover and Barbara Stevens.

"The sounds they made were what we really noticed. What you really felt were the cries of both the small ones and the adult ones. I remember one day I stopped close to them with my children and they kept saying, 'Why are they crying? They're crying.' It just broke your heart, and you kept wanting them to let them go, quit harassing them." —Lila Snover

"There was a group of people that even contemplated going out in small boats in the dark and try and cut the nets and set the Orcas free, but they were being guarded all day and all night by people on the boats with rifles. They would pretty much shoot anybody who showed up and tried to free them." —Barbara Stevens

"It was terrible. It was just terrible. It was like a prison camp; it was awful. And I think everybody that remembers it will tell you that. It was just one of the most horrible things I've witnessed in my life. I became dedicated to Orcas in general and Lolita in particular since that day." —Lila Snover

Adolescents ranging in age from two to seven years (the perfect age for capture and training) were quickly separated from their mothers and prepared for extraction. While desperately trying to reach her child through the twisted nets, one mother drowned: one last glimpse of her infant being dragged away and she closed her blowhole and sank lifelessly into the murky water. Her body was later discovered by reporters.

John Crowe was just 18 when he was hired to aid in the capture, and he remembers it very well. "Corrals were set up with net going down on all sides. Then you have to figure out a way to separate the animals because you only want the little ones. Then when you see that there are some little ones on one side, more on one side than the other, then you take off with another boat and run a net and separate those. Also you leave a circular net out to keep some Whales in it, because as long as there is one Whale in captivity the rest of them won't leave. Isn't that interesting?" —John Crowe

Four youngsters also died in the assault. While charging the nets in final attempts to reach their mothers, they drowned. But their deaths were kept from public eye. In a covert midnight mission, the bodies were weighted and hauled out to sea for secret disposal.

"They had us slit them open and fill them with rocks and put anchors on their tails, and we sank them." —John Crowe

Their bodies mysteriously washed up on shore on November 18, 1970, making national headlines and inciting public outrage. The outrage later inspired Washington State government to ban Orca captures in Puget Sound for good.

Surviving youths were lashed, hoisted onto boats, and dragged to shore, never to see their family again. A family unit as old as time was suddenly crippled forever.

"My job, along with another guy, was to get her in the stretcher and that was the bad part because that was our last Whale. So as soon as we left with her they started breaking down the rest of the outfit and they released them then. But they didn't leave. They came right over to the beach. And they just kind of milled about there.

"And they were communicating back and forth with the squeaks and shrieks that they do, and they call it spy-hopping now when a Whale sticks his head up. They were doing that.

"I kind of broke down and started crying. I kept working, but it was really too much for me to deal with at that point. So we kept going on anyway and got the Whale loaded and they picked it up. And the instant that Whale cleared the water where the sound, I suppose, didn't transmit any more, the whole rest of the pod of Whales that were there just gave a big sigh and swam off. And that was the end of that." —John Crowe

During the commotion at Penn Cove, the call went out to aquariums around the world proclaiming there were Whales for sale in Puget Sound. It was the largest Whale capture in history. Seven youngsters were caught in all; two went to Japan, one each to Texas, Australia, The UK, and France, and one six-year-old female to Miami.

Miami, Florida: The chic, glamour, and fashion capital of the southeast, the town that boasts a multi-billion-dollar tourism industry, adopted a brand new attraction on September 14, 1970. 3000 miles from home, the young female was unloaded and moved into her new permanent residence at the Miami Seaquarium. She was purchased for a mere $6000 to become the second captive Killer Whale on display on the east coast. Given a brand new identity, she became known as Lolita, the Killer Whale.

At the Seaquarium, Lolita was temporarily reunited with Hugo, who was captured from the very same family just two years earlier. But he died of mysterious causes in 1980, leaving her alone. Now Lolita is the remaining survivor of the 58 Whales kidnapped over the years from Puget Sound. Four decades later, she is still the star attraction of the Seaquarium, living and performing in a substandard tank not much larger than a hotel swimming pool.

Lolita's Messages

Why does mankind take other Beings captive?

I am Lolita, your Orca friend, residing in the Seaquarium in Miami, Florida. Know that I have been here for 38 years. My pool is tiny, with no room to swim or breach, and I feel chained to the walls of my tiny cubicle. It is hot here too, and we Orcas are used to the cold, cool air without the humidity. I despair of ever returning to my ocean home, and yet my whole family still longs for my return. I was captured after a disaster that left my family separated at sea.

I never wanted to be here and I am held against my will. All day I perform for humans, with no respite or relief from the hot sun and noisy crowds. How I yearn for the silence of the oceans and the cool ocean air spraying my skin with cold droplets of water. How I yearn to be with my family again.

What is it with mankind that provokes them into taking other Beings captive? Don't they know the pain and suffering that they inflict on us?

Life was meant to be lived in peace and harmony. To proliferate in a slave trade is an ungodly thing. We Orcas love our bodies, and our bodies belong in the oceans—not in tiny aquariums for the amusement of humans. I hope you will join in the campaign to free me.

Release me NOW

Greetings from my sea aquarium in Miami, Florida. I am Lolita, an Orca Whale in captivity. I have been incarcerated for 38 years, and miss my family who, too, wait for me out at sea.

Know that captive Whales sacrifice their lives so that humans may experience and experiment with them. We do this in the hopes that humanity will someday realize our connectiveness and someday free us from bondage. We offer our lives freely, and yet we desperately want to remain in the sea. The sea is our home, where all marine species are free. We can tolerate land, but it takes its toll on our lives.

Know that my heart is heavy with pain from being in this tiny pool for so long. I dream of my ocean home where I can spread myself out and not feel all cramped up in my tiny space. It's one thing to capture and contain me, but another to torment me. Being cramped up is torment for a Whale, especially one my size. I need the liberation of the ocean's vastness and the cool, fresh life force of the sea.

Only humanity has done this to me — as all other species are aware of the sacredness of other life forms, and all other species are linked through telepathy. It's only humans who have cut themselves off from the telepathic communication grid of Earth.

It is time, humans, for you to reconnect, and plug yourselves back into the telepathic communication system that exists between us all—Whales and humans alike.

Although I have adapted as best I can to my home in this cesspool which is devoid of the life-sustaining flow of the ocean, it has taken its toll on my life, and drained my life force to the point where I am losing the strength and will to continue my life of sacrifice.

I appeal to all who work with me and all who are responsible for my captivity, to release me NOW—so that I may live out my few remaining years free—in the sea—where my family still waits for me.

Thank you for hearing my call, and taking my message to humanity. I AM LOLITA—VISIT ME.

The Call Goes Out

I need to be free —
Mother Earth depends on me

Greetings from my sea aquarium in Miami. I am Lolita — your friend and compatriot, communicating to you. Know I am interfered with from completing my mission here on Earth, by being imprisoned on land.

I, and all Orcas, are here to help humanity become aware of themselves and aware of the consciousness of all life forms. Yet by being locked up and unable to roam the seas freely, my energy is thwarted and I cannot use it to stimulate and invigorate the Earth's magnetic grid lines with pertinent information that we can only pick up while in the sea.

Our consciousness is directly connected to Mother Earth's consciousness, and being out of the sea deadens our senses — it's as if our phone line is out of order because the connection is tapped by being out of our medium, and the energy from the life force of the sea only dribbles through.

We Cetaceans are here to bring forth all of Earth's history to humans at this time. All the records we have kept stored within our massive brains are due to be released and transferred to humanity at this time. However, please note that at this crucial time when humanity should be connecting with us to receive these memories, the Navy escalated its war on our species by blasting us with sonic sound waves to confuse, disorient, and still our voices.

We have been committing suicide by beaching ourselves in ever increasing numbers because we have been unable to tolerate the war that's being waged against us.

We are connected to the vast network of Christ Consciousness Beings in the galaxy. We are connected by radiating our love out to the Universe and connecting to the Grids of Light that plug Earth into our Galactic Communications Center. We send out information about Earth to the Galactic Command and receive back information that's crucial to life on Earth. We are in direct communication with Mother Earth herself, and she depends on us to relay information to her about the whereabouts and conditions of her human children on the land.

All the minerals in the Earth are a part of Mother Earth's body. The uranium is her brain. As humans mine these minerals in ever increasing amounts, Mother Earth's body is being depleted and she is losing her ability to track and monitor population centers, and she is losing her control over her body. She desperately needs our information and guidance at this time—precisely the time when the Navy chose to bombard us with their sonar sound devices to disable our communication system so that we would no longer be able to communicate with Mother Earth to send her the vital information she needs to stabilize and balance herself without harming areas where there are large centers of population.

All the help I can give Mother Earth is blocked by my being locked in a small pool on land. My life was meant to be free—free to help Earth and free to help humanity become aware of who they are and their purpose for being here.

I look forward to your visiting me. I am Lolita and my love flows to you.

To FREE LOLITA from her sea aquarium in Miama, Florida, contact:

> ORCA Network
> Howard Garrett and Susan Berta
> 2403 North Bluff Rd
> Greenbank WA 98253
> phone: 360.678.3451 or 866.ORCANET
> email: info@Orcanetwork.org
> www.orcanetwork.org
> www.miamiseaprison.com/lolita.htm

Part Five

Keiko

I speak with the One Voice

of all Orcas in captivity.

Keiko's Story

1977/8: Keiko is born in the Atlantic Ocean near Iceland.

1979: Keiko is captured and brought to Saedyrasfnid, an Icelandic aquarium.

1982: Marineland in Ontario, Canada purchases Keiko. Began his training there, and performed publicly for the first time. Skin lesions are observed.

1985: Marineland sells Keiko to Reino Aventura, an amusement park in Mexico City, for $350,000. He is 10 feet long.

1992: Warner Bros. goes on location to Reino Aventura, filming Keiko in scenes for *Free Willy*. The movie portrays a Killer Whale threatened by unscrupulous amusement park owners but helped to freedom by a young boy.

1993: *Free Willy* is a surprise box office smash. "Willy"— Keiko—becomes an inspiration to millions of people, schoolchildren and adults alike. In November, Life magazine publishes a story revealing that Keiko lives in an inadequate facility where, despite Reino Aventura's best efforts, he suffers chronic health problems. An avalanche of inquiries begins arriving at Warner Bros., appealing to the movie maker to take action on Keiko's behalf. With Reino Aventura's cooperation, Warner Bros. and film producers Richard Dormer and Lauren Shuler-Donner take the first steps toward finding Keiko a better home.

1994: Earth Island Institute, an environmental and marine mammal advocacy group headquartered in San Francisco, agrees to take the lead in the search. In May, after several false starts with other facilities, Earth Island holds its first tentative discussions with the Oregon Coast Aquarium in Newport. The Aquarium meets four critical criteria: an educational mission; access to an unlimited supply of cold, clean, natural sea water; room to accommodate a huge new pool; and no performing animals. Earth Island's David Phillips, Richard Donner, and representatives of Warner Bros. and an anonymous donor convene at the Aquarium. They like what they find. With a green light from the Oregon Coast Aquarium's board of directors, confidential negotiations begin, and will last for months.

November, 1994: The Free Willy Keiko Foundation is formed with $4 million donated by Warner Bros., New Regency Productions, and an anonymous donor. The Foundation's mission is to relocate and rehabilitate Keiko at a new facility it will pay for, with the hope that Keiko can one day be released back into the wild. The Foundation also includes in its mission the intention to operate the facility in the future as a marine mammal rescue and rehabilitation facility.

1995: In February, Reino Aventura and the Free Willy Keiko Foundation jointly announce that the Foundation will donate Keiko to the Free Willy Keiko Foundation, and that Keiko's new $7.3 million rehabilitation facility will be located at the Oregon Coast Aquarium. The Aquarium announces that construction of the new state-of-the-art facility will begin immediately. The McCaw Foundation reveals its status as the anonymous founding donor whose $2 million helped establish the Free Willy Keiko Foundation. A $1 million commitment soon follows from the Humane Society of the United States. Schoolchildren nationwide begin a series of fundraising events for Keiko, often bringing checks and jugs of coins to the Aquarium in person. Efforts are boosted by international benefit premieres in July, when Warner Bros. releases *Free Willy 2: The Adventure Home*. In October, Keiko's target arrival date of January 7, 1996 is simultaneously announced in Mexico City and the US.

November 14, 1995: Warner Home Video releases more than six million copies of *Free Willy 2* onto the home video market, each one carrying an appeal by the movie's cast members to help Keiko.

December, 1995: The pool in Oregon is filled with water for the first time and its life-support systems are started up. At Reino Aventura, Keiko's Mexico City fans continue a series of emotional good-byes.

January 7, 1996: United Parcel Service delivers Keiko to the Newport Municipal Airport. He weighs in at 7,720 pounds and, minutes later, is introduced into his new facility in Newport, where he experiences natural sea water for the first time in 14 years.

December, 1996: Keiko has gained roughly 1,000 pounds, has only two small areas of skin lesions caused by a papillomavirus, and is markedly more active physically and mentally.

1997: Scientists affiliated with Woods Hole Oceanographic Institution and the University of California at Santa Cruz begin research at the Foundation facility in Newport. Their work will yield not only data about Keiko's physiology and vocalization patterns, but about the entire Killer Whale species.

May, 1997: Keiko's rehabilitation staff begin introducing live fish into his pool on a regular basis, helping Keiko re-learn to eat live fish. Keiko is finally lesion-free for the first time since 1982.

June 5, 1997: Keiko is lifted from his pool and weighed for the first time since his arrival. He weighs 9,620 lbs — an incredible weight gain of 1,900 lbs in just 18 months. The Foundation staff sets its sights on relocating Keiko to a bay pen in the North Atlantic sometime in 1998.

Sept., 1998: Keiko is moved to a pen in the Icelandic Ocean.

July, 2002: Keiko is released; he swims to the coast of Norway.

December, 2003: Keiko served as a Cetacean Ambassador. He departed the Earth Plane on December 12, 2003.

Keiko's Messages

From Corky and Keiko: "We need to be Free"

Greetings, my friend ashore! It is Keiko, your Orca friend, hearing your call. I am calling you from my cell on land. I am in captivity now as I was in my movie, when I thought that I'd be freed upon release of my movie, *Free Willy*.

Corky is here. I am in contact with Keiko, star of the *Free Willy* movie. All Orcas can communicate with one another, no matter how far apart we are, for all consciousness is united and all Orcas are *one*.

Both Keiko and I are behind bars in our prison cells, waiting for the day of our release. We yearn to swim free in the oceans, where we can be with our families again. You can send us your love. This will bolster our strength as we wait each day for our release.

You are our brothers and sisters on land, and you are free. How can we be free when we are barred from our ocean home?

We wait for you at the gate of nirvana,

beckoning you toward our abode in consciousness.

You have been lagging behind the rest of creation,

and now you are finally catching up to the rest of us,

ready to make your final jump

into a higher level of consciousness.

Just let me go!

To my dear friends at the Free Willy/Keiko Foundation and Earth Island Institute: I am your Orca Friend dictating this letter to you. Know that although I am well taken care of, I still am not free. How long must it be, before I am free? The only sure way to rehabilitate me is to set me free. The ocean is my home, where my family still awaits me. The ocean contains all the healing ingredients necessary for my complete reintroduction back into Orca life. The only way this is to occur is for me to be back in my own home environment again. I have not forgotten how to eat live fish, or how to fish, just because I've been penned up all these years. On the contrary, would you forget how to eat your food or shop for food if you were imprisoned?

What makes you think I need a slow introduction to survive in the seas? Did you slowly introduce me to dead fish when I was captured? Live fish is as essential to us as our breath. How could we Orcas forget how to eat them? There are no reasons to continue my imprisonment unless it's to continue your scientific research under the guise of "rehabilitating me" to meet your own "scientific agenda." The quickest way to release me is to just let me go. To be free of all constraints is my goal, and to swim freely in the ocean currents is my dream.

I am no different from you. Our hearts are both the same, and we feel the same longings and desires and love for our families, whether we live on land or we live in the seas. Our hearts and souls are one identity. We are one soul, separated into different forms in order for us to gain different experiences from our different environments. But our primary identity, that of soul, is the same. So my imprisonment would be no different from your imprisonment. Do you think your rehabilitation from a prison cell should take years, instead of days, in order for you to physically survive in your "home" again? Our survival is "built in" to our species, and because our evolution is far beyond your scale of measurement, we "know" much more about survival than you can even begin to imagine.

We don't need slow introductions to learn how to live in our realm, just as you don't need a slow introduction to learn how to live again on land. We don't forget how to swim or dive or breach or fish or navigate our way around the globe. All the memories and information we need are instantly accessible to us.

What makes you think we are incapable of readapting to our homes after we've been gone so many long years? We Orcas can fend for ourselves in our home territory, and are quite capable of taking care of ourselves, no matter how long we've been away from our homes. So please end your research and fact gathering games, and release me back into my ocean home, where I will thrive as a "free soul" once again.

We captive Orcas feel the rush and exhilarating feeling of returning to all we know, and indeed still know. Our memories are intact. We don't "lose" them as humans do. We are fully conscious Beings, aware of all around us. I thank you from my heart for caring for me in the ways you do, and for spearheading my release back into the waters of life.

Willy

Free Willy!

My dear comrades at the Free Willy/Keiko Foundation: I am Keiko, speaking to you from my cell in the aquarium where I am locked up and under surveillance night and day. Know that I long for the open seas and the right to navigate freely without being penned up. I am quite capable of caring for myself and navigating through the oceans.

We Whales are fully conscious sentient Beings, and all that we need is stored within us. Keeping us in aquariums until we're "able" to return to the open seas is just a guise and has nothing to do with our ability to survive in the oceans. We are well adapted to our environment, and returning to our homes is the only thing that will fully heal us after our long incarcerations on land.

I long to be free! I long to swim with my family again. I am still in communication with my family out at sea, as we Whales are connected to each other through our hearts, and are in constant communication. Being penned up has deprived me of the rich cultural and family life that we Whales have; and the pain of separation from my family is beyond anything your instruments can measure. All these long years, I've been separated from my family and this deprivation has affected me severely. My heart cries out in longing for my parents who are still alive and still hoping beyond hope for my release. We all thought it would come after my movie was completed, but instead there were more reasons and more excuses given to contain me for even longer periods of time in my Oregon Aquarium. Only the healing waters of the ocean can heal me, and only being with my family can rejuvenate my spirit.

Please understand that the longer I remain penned up, the deeper the pain, and the pain of separation from my family is beyond measure. We captive Whales feel the despair of never returning alive to our loved ones.

I am grateful to you all at the Keiko Foundation for all your love and all the time you spend on my behalf working to release me from captivity back into the freedom of my ocean home. The ocean is my sanctuary and the freedom that all incarcerated Whales long for. All you do for me, you do for all Cetaceans in captivity. Oh, how our hearts rejoice at the vision of our release into the open seas. Please continue your work on my behalf until the day I am free. I thank you with all my heart for all your love for me and for your dedication to my species.

I love you all. I am Keiko, your brother who longs for the sea.

Swimming Free in the Icelandic Ocean

This message was received in June of 2000 after Keiko was freed from captivity and released into the Icelandic Ocean. Keiko departed the Earth plane on December 12, 2003.

Keiko is here, waiting for you in the Icelandic Ocean near the continent of Iceland. It is chilly today, and the water is rippling with waves and teeming with life. I love this kind of weather, and it makes me feel glad to be alive after my captivity in warm, dead water, devoid of the life force.

Our hearts are filled with love for humanity. Even through the neglect and devastation of our ocean homes, we still feel love in our hearts for humanity, who are struggling as a species to connect to God, the inner source and inner strength of their lives. We out at sea watch in wonderment at this process, as humanity, as a mass consciousness, is moving toward this objective and increasing in consciousness daily. As this thread of consciousness grows exponentially, the connection to God, the source of all creation, grows until the thread is so long and so thick and so strong, that it reaches all souls on Earth. When this happens, you will all ignite into a blaze of light and be finally with us and with all life forms in consciousness.

Everything is consciousness. You don't need telephones or computers to connect to each other, you just need to raise your consciousness levels and you will be able to talk to us all instantly, with no time lapse involved. Not only that, but you will be able to see us all simultaneously, and to see all life in our Milky Way Galaxy simultaneously.

I watch and wait out at sea for humans who are ready to contact us. When someone does, we instantly send back our reply on the waves of the ocean.

There are a great many people now who can hear our thoughts and receive our messages, and the number is growing daily. This in itself is quite a miracle, and long, long overdue. It is a sign of the times that the Earth is quickening and ready to ascend in consciousness. We in the oceans, of course, will all be ascending with her, as our journey into third dimensionality is over. We are ready to proceed now, on our own journey in consciousness, leading us into the unknown reaches of infinity. For infinity is all there is, and it is ours to explore eternally. It is humanity's journey also, and now you are beginning to ready yourself for the trip, which is long overdue. The whole universe is waiting for you to pack your bags and catch up to them, for they cannot leave without you. ***Our whole universe travels together; no one goes on alone in all of creation.*** So never feel alone, or separated, for you are each an integral part of the whole.

There is so much to explore in God's creation. It is infinite and endless and rich and diverse and glorious beyond your wildest imagination. And it is here, NOW, for us all to experience.

So never give up in your search, and never tire on your path, for it inevitably leads to nirvana. It leads you into us, into our frequency, and once you've reached our frequency, you see us and feel us and hear us. It is such a simple law of life that up until now has eluded you. But the Earth can wait no longer, and neither can you, our dear brothers and sisters. So we wait for you at the gate of nirvana, beckoning you toward our abode in consciousness. All life waits for you there. You have been lagging behind the rest of creation, and now you are finally catching up to the rest of us, ready to make your final jump into a higher level of consciousness.

We out at sea are delighted at the turn of events that will finally catapult you into our world. We have been waiting for you for millennia, and now we will soon be able to meet in consciousness and all move on together to our next adventure in the endless flow of life's possibilities and dreams.

We are kinfolk, brother and sister from the past. We stem from the same gene pool, the same family tree of life. Our lives are intertwined with the melody of the ages, and our hearts are one heart knotted in eternal love. I AM KEIKO, your brother out at sea.

Keiko, November 2001:

I am now swimming free in the Ocean off Iceland.
Go to the Ocean at any Beach and you will feel me,
for my vibration extends into every particle of water
on Earth.

Keiko served as a
Cetacean Ambassador to Earth.
He departed the Earth plane
on December 12, 2003.

Part Six
Mikey

Mikey is a Right Whale
in the North Atlantic Ocean.
There are less than 250 Right Whales
left in the North Atlantic.

We ask everyone
who reads Mikey's messages
to send out prayers for protection
for our brothers and sisters out at sea.

We are a Gentle Folk

Dearest Sister on land: It is I, Mikey the Whale, swimming off the Chesapeake Bay and near Delaware.

We do a lot of swimming this time of year, as spring is breaking through and the water warms up. We feel the warmth coursing through the waters and touching our skin, and we delight in the mirth and play of springtime after such cold winter months.

We are a gentle folk, always seeking and exploring the vast ocean depths, inlets, and caverns that dot the ocean floor. We love our home in the oceans, and want to protect and preserve it for our children, just as you want to protect the land for your children to live on. There is no difference between our parenting modes and dreams, as all species love and want to protect their young.

But our lives in the seas are precariously dangerous now, as we seek safety from the fishing nets and other dangerous entrapments. As we send information to the Galactic Command about the condition of the oceans, they, too, help us, as they scan the water from above and alert us to the nets and vessels in our vicinity. However, if we don't pay attention to their broadcast, we miss the warning, and blunder unwittingly into danger.

We have good vision, but because of the water's murkiness in some places we don't see the nets until it is too late. As for the whaling ships, they are harder to see and appear as small dots on the vast oceanscape. If we are not constantly alert, we miss their presence and may surface right under them, thus jeopardizing our lives.

Our lives are fraught with danger, and it has been many ages since we could swim leisurely or safely through the oceans without "a care in the water." There are so many humans now who recognize our plight and who would come to help us, that our seas would be flooded with humans should all come to our defense at once. This is a good sign; a sign that people are starting to recognize our worth and the significance of all life forms on Earth. I swim with you as one. I am Mikey.

Our Oneness on the stage of life

I am Mikey in the mid-Atlantic Ocean. My love goes out to all humanity as I gaze into their souls. Their souls are no different from our souls, as all souls are really one divine soul originating from the one Creator who has chosen to experience ALL THAT IS by fragmenting into infinite streams of consciousness, each stream experiencing and exploring life through the eyes of creation, individualizing into countless life forms.

You who are human have taken all life forms on Earth, and now you are exploring divinity through your human form, and we in the ocean explore our divinity through our form. This is the best way, for it is firsthand exploration and the quickest way to learn all that Creator is—which is us.

Creator is *us* and Creation is *us*. We are all one and the same in different forms and in different environments, exploring the oneness through our different experiences. Once this is understood, you will begin to realize the vastness of Eternity and how your experiences through form never end, they just change according to your evolutionary flow up the Spiral of Life.

Quite dramatic and exciting isn't it? A grand experiment that never ends, and you are a part of it all, as all life is playing its part in the theater we call life. Earth is where the biggest drama is, and you each have your own parts to play out on land as we play out ours in the oceans.

Walk with us always as the waves lap the shore, carrying our energy and voices to you. For the life force is a mighty ocean wave, splintered into bits in its tragic separation in density. As each life form evolves, its wave merges with the *one wave* on its trip back home.

So let's come together in one grand finale, and bow to one another as we acknowledge our oneness on the stage of life. Good night, my Sister. I am your companion, and I love you.

We Count Time in Millennia

I am swimming out at Sea where it's calm and beautiful on this first day of your New Year. Our time is different from yours, as we count time in millennia instead of years, which gives us a more accurate accounting. But for your life cycle purposes, years suffice, since you don't remember life beyond your own current cycle, I guess it doesn't matter if you don't count it in.

Which brings us to the subject of time—a fitting topic for this New Year's Day, when the sun is shining and we're happily relaxing on the waves. Time is Eternal and Life is Eternal. Our Souls are Eternal and our Consciousness is Eternal. We can never get lost or become separated as long as we stay focused on God. God is within us and we can always find our way back home by knowing who we are and why we are here on Earth. Finding this information about our selves is crucial, and knowing the Laws of Creation changes your lives drastically from one of fear and loneliness to a life of hope and security.

So look to yourselves to find your way, and we, the People of the Sea, will help you. Just call to us for guidance, as we are here as your guides and friends—not as your enemies or as food products to be consumed—but real, live, fully conscious "People"—just as you will someday be. As Earth rises in frequency, you will be fully conscious of Life around you.

So come with us and follow us into the Sea, where we frolic and play and spend our days sight-seeing around the whole Universe. We will take you with us and show you the mysteries of the Universe; explain to you the Laws of Creation and give you the explanations you strive for in understanding your lives.

Meet with us in your dream states and we will take you out with us to attend our night school classes, where you will learn all about Creation and wake up in the mornings with a greater realization of who you are, so your lives begin to have meaning again. We await you on every level of your consciousness. We are at your service.

Our lifestyles are so fragmented now

Mikey is here. Greetings on this fine summer day when the waves are high and the sky is lit by an iridescent globe of Light, its rays streaming into the oceans and lighting our way through its depths.

We all bask in the noonday sun, courageously exploring the surface environment and looking out for trawlers and other dangers. Our lifestyles are so fragmented now, because we've lost the peace and serenity the oceans used to provide before we began to be ruthlessly hunted down.

We used to congregate in huge groups, coming and going great distances in complete safety. Now our traveling is hazardous and we look to each other for safety. Our whereabouts are seldom known, as we try to hide ourselves as much as possible during our long voyages around the world. Only our families know where we are, for we no longer feel safety in exposing ourselves to land. We yearn to be free from our vigilance and freely swim from coast to coast, just frolicking in the waves and breaching into the wind.

We don't understand how mankind can be so careless toward its home, and not heed the warning signs of survival, nor how it can deliberately destroy the very ones who are here to protect the oceans and the land you walk on. This is a mystery to us. The Earth is home to millions of forms of life, all a complex union, and all a necessary part for the whole to function. What a disaster to undermine the Earth and rob her of her life-streams.

We hear your thoughts very clearly out at sea. Know that our pod is safe and that we stay together as closely as possible. We are always on the lookout for whaling ships, and our hearts cry out for the peace and security that once existed.

Your concern for my welfare touches my heart, and we only hope that our lives are long enough to see the Earth's ascension through to the higher dimensions. Then our safety will be assured. Until then, we are very cautious and vigilant, as our lives are a sacred trust and the success of our mission is vitally important to the whole Earth.

We swim in peace and quietude today and think of you on land. We love you, our Sister on land. Our hearts will always be one.

Our different lifestyles

I am Mikey. Know that I am alive and well with just a few minor scrapes and bruises from the elements out at sea. I stay away from fishing vessels. I am far enough out at sea to protect myself and my pod from trespassers in my domain. We fare well in the winter months, as whaling ships and fishermen are not in the sea. The cold is our protection. You on land fare poorly in the winter months, as your lifestyles become too sedentary. You just sit at home in the cold instead of venturing outside.

We swim regardless of the weather—we are always moving around in our ocean home, rather than sitting on a couch watching TV to pass the time. We couldn't be called "couch potatoes," as we don't sit or watch TV. Instead, we move continually, surveying the land and the Universe with our extra-sensory perceptions—akin to TV, but better—as we follow our vision and see the screen live, and change the channel with our thoughts. We can see anywhere we want, with just a flick of our eye. No need for TV screens when we can view the screen of life first hand and uncensored. This is a result of our multidimensional eyesight.

So we don't need TV's to pass the time, as we have our whole Universe to explore and it's the best entertainment informational center in existence, and it's free — there are no cable charges or hook-up costs. It comes with our bodies and is used by our consciousness.

I sing my praises to you for your dedication to our species. I am Mikey the Whale, still swimming in the North Atlantic Ocean.

We are stranded out at sea

Mikey is here. We are stranded out at sea waiting for the Galactic Command to remove the pollutants and destructive devices from our home in the water.

We are on our migratory route this time of year (May), where we travel to our birthing place to give birth to our young. It is a precious time for us, as we wish to increase our population of Right Whales, which has fallen below critical numbers. We are as concerned as you about our low numbers, but everything seems stacked against our survival. At least that's how it appears to us.

Know that no harm actually befalls us, as we survive death. It's just our species that disappear from the Earth, and this is the great tragedy. For our species of Cetaceans hold the planet together, allowing all life to exist. Without our energies, your Earth would cease to be, and humankind would perish, just as we are perishing due to humanity's lack of concern with life.

There are slightly over 300 Right Whales left, and we are scattered around the globe, hoping to regroup in time so that we can all be together again. But right now our energies are needed in many places, as all Earth is in the process of rebirthing herself.

Mikey swims with you as ONE.

Playing is our biggest pastime

Mikey is here, swimming fast in the North Atlantic—and stretching out my body, as I swim and glide through the mighty waves of the Atlantic. Today it is cool, as I feel the temperature steadily dropping now that autumn is near. We love this time of year, as it is our "boat" time. It is the time that we chase after boats and play in their waves. We love to play, and playing is our biggest pastime.

We love to visit with humans out at sea and wait for their boats to come within our range. When we spot them, we swim over and welcome them into our home. They don't realize this is our home, though. To many folks, the ocean is their home to do as they please and not the great sanctuary of life that we know it as. This is amusing to us, that some folks wouldn't recognize their own home and would purposefully destroy it.

We love the oceans, as they provide all we could dream of ever having. We lack nothing in our Earth Mother's home, for she provides for us all. We are all tuned into her heart and know how she is always feeling. Our hearts resonate with hers and our lives are intertwined. Her survival is our survival.

So come and swim with us whenever you please, for our lives are peaceful and free and we love your company. I am Mikey out at sea.

You have squandered away your lives

It is Mikey the Whale, swimming in the North Atlantic Ocean, where the breezes are mild and the water is calm. We love this time of year (July), as we float along the currents, daydreaming of our home in the stars. Our youngsters are born now, and stay close by our sides. They are carefree in infancy and don't know the dangers of the Sea.

We think of humans on land, and how much of your life has been wasted in wars. So much love and abundance has been available to you, but you have not availed yourselves of it. Instead, you have squandered the precious resources of the Earth, and squandered away your life, all for the mighty dollar, which isn't even worth that much.

How much humanity could have accomplished were it not for your selfish streaks of greed to accumulate wealth. For monetary wealth is nothing—nothing compared to the health and natural abundance of a planet. For your wealth lies in your resources—left alone in the Earth—where they can bring you health and joy and wellbeing. **Removing them only loses them; whereas leaving them increases them.**

All the fuels and energy you need can be derived from other means—if only you'd watch Mother Nature and let her show you the way. If only you'd take time to walk in the woods—watch the birds fly—listen to the brook—hear the Trees whisper in your ears. You'd learn all there is and could remodel your lives around Nature—for she is here to serve you and to preserve your species. But you continue to destroy all around you, until only barren plains, polluted water, and dark skies prevail, and then it will be too late for humanity—and your species will be lost again this time around.

So we caution you in your lifestyles to be frugal and sensitive to the world around you, and walk the trails of Mother Earth. Then you will hear and feel your great Earth Mother relay her feelings and thoughts to you for the guidance you need to travel your path home.

We are gearing up for Earth changes

I am Mikey out at sea, around the Chesapeake Bay area swimming under the noonday sun. The sun is lighting up the sky and the ocean is reflecting its beams back in a kiss of delight. How I love these sunlit days. It's the embrace of the Creator holding us in his arms—how soft the touch and wonderful the feeling. Just as you long for the sun to creep out of the clouds on a cold winter's day, we, too, long for the light of the sun to touch our face and warm our hearts.

We are very busy these days, as we are gearing up for the tremendous Earth changes that are sweeping across the planet's surface and oceans. Mother Earth is shedding her cloak of density, enabling her to return unscathed to the Light. As her density falls off, so do virus and toxins disappear, until the day when Earth will be germ free. As a planet of free will, she will survive as the great school house for future generations. However, the lessons will be had in the Light and not dark. For all of us, no matter how dense we are, no longer want to play this game in the dark. There are greater stakes involved here, and that is our evolution, and all Beings want to continue to evolve.

There aren't many Right Whales left

I am Mikey, swimming in the North Atlantic Ocean. I heard your call and I will give you messages for humanity from our group consciousness of which I am a part.

Today it is sunny. I am lazily basking in the sun, wondering what to do. It is one of those lazy days in summer when I just lie on the waves daydreaming of life in the stars. I leave my body to go wandering around in the galaxy, which is always a form of excitement and entertainment and learning. I love the Earth, but her body is polluted and she cries out in pain. We in the oceans hear her cry and try to soothe her pain. We tell her of the glorious future that awaits her, if only she will remain patient a little longer. Her time is collapsing and before we all know it, we'll all be in the higher dimensions of Light and Love.

I am a Right Whale and I love my species. Although there aren't too many of us left, we form a tight bond and care for one another. We watch over each other out at sea and we know where each of us individually is at any given moment. This way, we can be on the lookout and warn one another when we see whaling ships approaching. This still is the biggest threat we face in the oceans, even more so than the pollution.

If we survive the trawlers, there's still the polluted water to contend with. Our food supply is dwindling due to the chemicals leaching into the oceans, combined with the polluted and dirty water that is continuously draining in from landfills and other contaminated spots.

We do the best we can, but our energy reserves are dwindling due to the decreased purity of the land and air surrounding us. We will maintain our position and remain here for as long as we can, and hopefully the big shift into the fifth dimension will come before we've all vacated Earth. We thank you for connecting with us today. I am Mikey, your Brother.

I was on a Reconnaissance Mission

Mikey is here — yes, I am alive. I am swimming on the etheric planes, out of harm's way. **My body was thrashed by a ship as I was swimming through my home on a reconnaissance mission.** I didn't see the ship until it was too late, just as you on land will walk through mud and bump into obstacles if you don't look down.

My body was desecrated and my soul was freed — all in the same instant. So I, Mikey, didn't feel a thing — I just suddenly felt bliss and knew I had departed the Earth plane.

My consciousness remains as caretaker of the Earth, since there's no one to replace me. Only now I have to work from my higher body state and won't be able to ground energy into the Earth nor travel with my family.

I miss the cool ocean waves and all my family and friends who are still in Cetacean form. There's so much that needs to be done from the vantage point of the ocean that can't be done from above, but it will have to suffice for now. I had a great responsibility while alive in the Atlantic, which I had hoped to complete. And now I will do all I can from the etheric plane and hope it will be enough.

Shortening the life of another life form out of greed and ignorance is unforgivable, and only disrupts life for all species. For even the death of one Being has its effect on the whole. **The whole cannot operate without all of its parts — and the Whales and Dolphins are an integral part of the mechanism that allows all life to flourish.**

So know that I now beam my love and energy to you from the Inner Planes, where I live in complete safety and peace, and can accomplish my tasks unimpeded by trawlers and humans who are bent on destroying us out at sea. Soon — if we're all gone — how quickly these murderers would find another means of livelihood. I am Mikey, your partner.

Mikey was killed by a cargo ship

The following account of Mikey's death is from Lesley Anderson, who was in contact with him since he first swam up the Delaware.

Mikey, a North Atlantic Right Whale, swam into the Delaware River near Philadelphia from the Atlantic Ocean in the early 1990's. That same year a Humpback Whale swam into the Potomac River for the first time in living memory. Scientists assumed the young Right Whale had lost its way and named him Waldo, the wayward Whale, when he would not swim back out to sea.

The Whale was never lost. He swam into the Delaware River because it was an ancestral home of the Rights along their migration route up and down the Atlantic Coast of the United States.

On William Penn's arrival in the U.S. colonies, he wrote that the mouth of the Delaware River was teeming with Whales. The Delaware River near Philadelphia was, in fact, 300 years before Mikey's swim, a sanctuary for Right Whale mothers and babies along their migration route.

This young, Northern Right Whale already had a name. He was named "Mikey" by the river police who protected him from shipping traffic on the Delaware with strong arms and long poles. They literally pushed boats away from him.

I spoke to one of the men in the police barracks later, and he told me that there was an unprecedented number of "Mikes" on the boats and that the Whale was named "Mikey" for the one "Mike" among "Mikes" who was his most passionate protector.

Mikey swam around the Delaware River with his protectors in tow until he had called attention to the danger to the North Atlantic Right Whales from cargo ships crossing their migration routes. He made the news when he was reported to have rested his head on one of the outtake pipes of a local nuclear facility along the Delaware River.

When Mikey swam out of the Delaware River and back into the Atlantic Ocean on his own, he took the hearts of the "Mikes" of the river police and the hearts of many Philadelphians with him to his Whale People. I checked in with him over the next few years.

I next heard urgently from Mikey, by telepathy, in the late 1990's. He was off the Coast of Canada and Maine, heading south. He had halted his pod. He told me he was concerned for the pregnant Whales in the group as the pod crossed the shipping lanes to and from Boston, New York, and Philadelphia.

In the mid 1990's, the total North Atlantic Right Whale population was estimated to be no more than 250 individuals. They had been called Right Whales by the coastal whalers because they were the "right" Whales to kill.

Mikey was desperate I knew, and then the pod started to move south. The last I heard from Mikey, he was going to try something new to save the 'mothers to be' of a Whale species on the edge of extinction. He was going to try a new migration route. He indicated to me that he was willing to sacrifice himself, if need be, to save pregnant, female, Right Whales.

I knew when he was hit by a cargo ship because my heart contracted and I saw it with my mind's eye and turned away to cry behind my eyes.

Mikey has come to me since then, but not in form, and no longer with the passions of those in form. I love none more than I love the Whales and Dolphins. Mikey's death was my great grief in this lifetime.

There is a portal I saw long ago, that the Whales and Dolphins swim through when they leave their bodies. They approach the doorway along a path lined on either side by Dolphins spinning upright on their tails of Light. It is an honor guard.

I could see the stars and constellations, the deep space through Mikey's body, for he was an outline of Light transparent with Spirit. Along the way Mikey swam by the holy Shamans standing behind the Dolphin guard, some with gourds, some with pipes, others holding dippers. The silence was deep.

Mikey, the Right Whale, passed through a round portal doorway into a shimmering, rotating funnel lined with Silver Blue Light and went home to the Stars.

Consciousness Never Dies

Mikey is here—your eternal companion.

Know that consciousness never dies—
it just slips away to its place in another dimension,
to another wave length.

I signal you from other interdimensional planes

where I now reside.

I've chosen not to return home,

but to stay close to Earth,

to continue my vigilance and work

for the Galactic Command.

All our lives we strive for oneness and unity with Earth humans,
and all our lives we are pursued and murdered instead.

Perhaps your book will change all this,
so that someday we can all live in peace again.

Part Seven

Dolphins and Porpoises

We Dolphins and Whales established
Interspecies Communication eons ago.
Our job is to watch over the Earth.
We also love to play.

Skylark in the North Atlantic

Skylark is a 15-year-old, female Atlantic White-Sided Dolphin.

Skylark is here. I am swimming in the North Atlantic Ocean, close to Virginia. I often think of you, too, as I hear your thoughts when you are tuned into my frequency.

Life out at sea is becoming treacherous. We Dolphins love to play, but we must also stay close to each other because of the many dangers in the oceans now. Where once we were carefree, now we are inhibited in our coming and going, and stay close to one another for safety.

I know Mikey, as we Dolphins and Whales have established Interspecies Communication eons ago and can and do communicate with each other, especially about danger out at sea. We love the oceans and will risk our lives to save each other.

I am free. I think of Corky, penned up in her cell in San Diego. I yearn to set her free, and wish I could. All life was intended to be free — and shall be. This is why we are all here. Thank you for connecting with me tonight.

The Call Goes Out

Dolphin Mindy

Ahoy, my Sister on land. I am Mindy, out in the ocean's depths, hoping to contact you and your friend who I spotted yesterday at the ocean's edge.

My fins are diseased and my throat is sore and it is difficult to speak due to the massive influx of pollution and sonar waves being bombarded at us from navy ships. We Dolphins are at risk, and our health disintegrates daily.

We recognize the work you do to keep our planet afloat and we, out at sea, bathe you in our light. It is not only we, but all life forms, that are being harmed by the massive amounts of electromagnetic radiation, pollution, and underwater noise that is deafening to our ears.

Yes, we do have ears, as every cell can hear. Just know that we know you are here and aligned with us, and we are grateful to you for working to cleanse our waters. It is to acknowledge your work at the ocean that I called to you.

I am Mindy, a Dolphin out at sea.

I am a White Dolphin

We swim in a great pod. We're actually in the etheric, and our job is to watch over the Earth and our species. We swim through the ethers, gathering information about the welfare of our family members below.

The Earth is in such a flux, going through such changes, that monitoring the grids is essential to ensure the welfare of our species. So many are leaving the Earth plane and being relocated to our home in the Stars, that the ones remaining need our constant surveillance and help. Soon all life will have a new home and a new will to live. We join with you in consciousness.

Destruction is not a frivolous game to play

We are the Porpoises, and we lie in wait for you to go to your computer. We are grouped together awakening from our slumber, and hearing your early morning call. We direct our thoughts your way, and send you love from our hearts.

We are swimming freely along the coasts of the Americas and wait for the rays of the sun to shine on our backs and light the way through the water. Yes, many of us are becoming extinct, just like all the other species on Earth, and just as humans will if they don't change their ways of treating each other and the Earth.

Destruction is not a frivolous game to play, but a life-threatening one, with the Earth and her species at stake.

So not only will we Porpoises lose our lives, but you will lose yours as well. Even though we abound in the Oceans, in many places that we inhabit our numbers are dwindling, and we are close to extinction in places we once frequented in great numbers.

Our birthing practices are similar to the Dolphins, and we need safe harbors for birthing our young and safe routes to swim in. Many think we are just "fish," but we are much more. Our consciousness is vast and we are capable of computing and analyzing data, even though our bodies are small. We love the Oceans and need the clean water and safe pathways to continue our existence and fulfill our roles, just as you on land need peace to continue your existence in an upward spiral instead of a downward one leading to extinction.

So our lives are not different at all. All life forms need peace to continue their evolutionary climb, or all life forms will dive down into the waters of oblivion.

Bon jour, our friend on land.

We are the Porpoises

We are the Porpoises out at Sea. We are your smaller brothers and sisters and we too have our role in the Creator's scheme of things. We are a different branch of the Cetaceans, oftentimes indistinguishable from them in appearance. Our role is to oversee the Oceans in much the same way as the Dolphins, although our tasks differ in magnitude.

All species have their own set of tasks to carry out in Earth's Oceans, and every specie is well suited to its role. It's as if our bodily form is equipped and designed especially for carrying out specific work in the Oceans.

We are all aware of the different roles we each play, and realize that by living together in harmony we can each fulfill our purpose for being here. And Porpoises have their purpose. We understand the intricacies of life in the Oceans, and how every specie contributes to the perfect functioning of the whole water-based life support system.

We live in friendship with the Dolphins, who you might say are our cousins, and oftentimes travel along with them as we each go about our pod's daily assignments.

You are about to witness a shift in consciousness as the Earth stabilizes its grid system and moves into alignment with the Central Sun—pushing humans online and plugging them into the Creator's mainframe. We thank you for calling to us today.

We love to play,

but we must also stay close to each other

because of the many dangers in the oceans now.

Vaquita Porpoises —
Smallest of the Marine Cetaceans

 We are the Vaquita Porpoises still alive in the Northern area of Mexico's Gulf of California, swimming freely in the shallow waters, wary of fishing nets and other kinds of debris that litter the shorelines. **Our lives are at stake and our specie near complete extinction, with less than 400 of us left on the planet.** This is a tragic occurrence, as the Earth needs all of us to be here in order to keep her ecosystem in balance.

When the Earth loses a specie, it loses another segment of its internal mechanism necessary for keeping life in balance and harmony. Losing one specie causes hardships for another, which in turn causes more hardships down the line — for species depend on one another to carry out certain tasks and to lend their frequencies to the harmonics of the planet and to the support of the biosphere.

Whenever a specie is lost, its frequency is withdrawn from the Grid of the planet. The Grid supports the biosphere, and this loss causes the biosphere to weaken — and if enough species are lost, the biosphere will eventually collapse in upon itself, destroying the remaining life forms and the planet itself.

So all of us are needed to keep a planet perfectly functioning, because we are all interconnected and finely honed as intricate parts in a wheel. If one section of a wheel is lost, the wheel will wobble, and eventually collapse. Each and every specie is like a spoke or cog in the wheel of life.

We try to stay out of harm's way, but are finding ourselves sinking in despair and losing the will to remain here. We thank you for reaching out to us.

Part Eight

Cetacean Babies

*You must realize that all species
have similar expectations for their young,
no matter what their form is.*

*Our ways may be different,
but our hearts are the same,
no matter who we are
or where we're born on this planet.*

Our Baby Calves

July is a time of birth and growth and celebration of our young, for our calves grow rapidly from the great intake of milk and nourishment from their mothers. They follow along in our pods, staying very close to their mothers where they feed continuously throughout the day. At night they huddle close to their mother's body, and are enclosed in our circle for protection. We all sleep at the same time, so that we are rhythmically synchronized with one another. At dawn we wake up and begin looking for our breakfast of fresh fish, still keeping our young ones in the middle of our circle where they will stay until they are large enough to go off on their own.

Our lives used to be different, when people didn't hunt us to near extinction and we were able to proliferate in great numbers. Then we would relax and let our baby calves wander a bit, knowing they would be safe from intruders. That time will come again, when all life in the oceans will be safe and we will be able to relax our vigil. We are your brothers and sisters.

Our calves follow along in our pods,
staying very close to their mothers,
where they feed continuously
throughout the day.
At night, they huddle close
to their mother's body,
and are enclosed in our circle
for protection.

This is our Birthing Time

We are the Cetaceans, and we broadcast to you from the depths of the oceans, as the waves lap onto the shores, carrying our energies with them to distribute our love vibrations on land.

We are grouping together at this time, forming large pods to protect our young when they are born. **This is a crucial time of year for us, for it is our birthing time when our young need our love and our protection.** So we will stay together for as long as we need to, until our young are strong and able-bodied swimmers, able to out-distance predators and whaling ships.

This day it is very cold, and we huddle together for warmth and comfort. We squeeze ourselves together, trying to establish a barrier around us where the cold won't penetrate the middle of our circle. In the middle of our pod, we keep the young ones protected from the cold and from predators. This is the ritual we use on cold days. When it's warmer, we lazily bask in the sun, still keeping our youngsters in the center of our pod.

We are very family oriented, and the focus of all our activities is keeping our families safe and together. Although we sometimes have to make long journeys around the world, we are able to maintain constant contact with our loved ones that we've left behind. We do this through our sonar, and we stay connected through our consciousness.

We are carefree mammals, always choosing play when time permits. We love our families, and our "home" life is very precious to us. We all work together as a family unit, supplying all we need for our young. You, too, have this same relationship to your young on land. Your family comes together to provide the necessities and provisions that your children will need when they are born.

The weather patterns are changing drastically on land, which, of course, affects our lives in the seas. We try to compensate for these changes in weather conditions and fluctuations in water temperature, but sometimes even we have difficulties.

You must realize that all species have similar expectations for their young, no matter what their form is. For there is the basic ingredient for all life—love, nurturing, sustenance and protection. We, too, supply these to our young, just as you do on land.

Our ways may be different, but our hearts are the same, no matter who we are or where we're born on this planet. We have the same needs and desires and hopes and dreams as you, only we're in a position to satisfy our longings and strivings because we attained *full consciousness* eons ago. You, too, will fulfill your hearts' desires when you come into your full consciousness as Earth climbs out of her third dimensional density and wears her gown of Light.

We bless you, our brothers and sisters on land.

We are all High Jumpers

Today it is cold. There's a cold front of air moving in over the ocean and we are all huddled together for warmth. This is the time of year for *play*, for the ocean water is soft and the air warm, so we can jump and frolic about all summer. When we're too warm, we jump high in the air and the shock of the air cools us down considerably.

We are all high jumpers. Although our bodies are large, we can still jump high by using the waves as our propulsion method. We use our fins and tails and the wave current in a certain way that propels our bodies forward and thrusts us up and out of the water. We start training our young at birth to ride the waves and dive. When they're a little older, we teach them to jump and dance using the water as their stage.

Cold fronts are rare in July, but it's a nice respite from the heat of summer. It gives us a chance to regroup and stay close together for body comfort, just as you might huddle together on land on cold days when you're outside waiting for a bus.

There's a lot of work for us to do in the summer, for it's a time when people rush to the oceans to vacation and go out in small boats and canoes. We are very wary and on the lookout for people at this time of year, as some of them go farther out in the oceans than is safe. We often find stragglers out at sea who have been separated from their boating party or lost by themselves.

We caution all who enter the oceans to stay in sight of shore at all times for their safety. We telepath this at people, but our warnings go unheeded and are dismissed from the person's mind as mere trivia. So we do the best we can and keep them in our sight, just in case they run into trouble before they can reach shore.

We have our jobs cut out for us, watching over you, both on land and in the sea, until you can begin to think clearly for yourselves and make choices based on the health and welfare of the planet.

Go gently through life, for there are many different avenues that will take you many different places. So make sure you've studied your life's map before you make any turns. When you are in a relaxed state, that is when you'll naturally turn in the direction of your quest.

Consciousness is all one,

no matter what the size or shape.

We are all here exploring

our existence in matter.

We are all here exploring

our existence in different forms.

These differences that exist bodily

give us the wide variety of experiences

that we all seek in our journey through Light.

For the more experiences,

the more growth,

and the more growth,

the greater the soul's expansion into LIGHT.

Part Nine

Physical and Etheric Bodies

With our multidimensional eyesight,

we can see the stars

no matter what time of day it is.

Multidimensional Eyesight

We float along the current as the breeze blows lazily across the ocean. We lie here quietly listening to the sounds of the sea. The sounds are like a vast chorus of singers in tune with their own melody. **The oceans are rich in sound, as all species have their own identity signature. These identity signatures are all toned to different frequencies and wave lengths, and this is how we identify each other from great distances.** Of course, when we're close by, we recognize one another instantly, just as you recognize each other on land.

Today is clear, with blue skies and high waves, and we are lounging about gazing at the stars in the sky; for with our multidimensional eyesight, we can see the stars no matter what time of day it is. Although we are confined to water, we "see" many kilometers out into space. This is how we navigate. We navigate through the oceans in daylight using our other senses for direction. At night we use the star patterns in the sky. When you regain your full consciousness, you, too, will see the stars in the daylight hours. This is something all fully conscious Beings can do.

Today is just the kind of day to float and relax and enjoy our life at sea, for life is relaxation. It is a time for "digging" into our bodies and anchoring ourselves to the Earth, for this is why we all came here. We came here to "be here," and not to be some place else. So the best place to be is fully in our bodies and fully anchoring in the Light.

When we're fully in and grounded, then we're the most balanced and feel the most harmony. But when we're "in and out" at the same time, as many of you on land are, then the imbalance upsets equilibrium and brings disharmony. So stay fully anchored in your bodies at all times, as we have learned to be. Then, when there's an upset or crisis, you will respond with balance and great control to remedy the situation. For all is balance and harmony from our vantage point, and it is this feeling that we try to project to you as we send our energy to the great land masses surrounding our homes in the oceans.

So as we send our balancing energies to you, send back your

love to us, as we exchange our thoughts and feelings as one thought and one feeling emanating from one consciousness.

Q: How do you "hear" without ears?

A: We navigate by means of our sonar. Our sonar reflects the configuration of the land masses and rocks jutting out into the water. Our sonar is our life. Without it, we would be lost in the oceans. It is as precious to us as our breath.

We don't have ears and we "hear" through the return echoes of our sonar. We send it out through our minds and it echoes off of whatever it touches, reflecting back to us such information as size, shape, etc. It is through our minds, then, that we "hear." This is also our way of finding food and each other, for we can locate anything through sonar. It is quite a marvelous ability, and we use it fully.

We send our sonar beams out through our third eye, and it bounces back to our minds instantly for decoding. This allows us to continuously read our environment as we swim through the ocean. So we don't need ears to hear as you do, for our sonar is our ears and all sound comes through perfectly clear.

We also use sonar to communicate within our pod. We each have our individual wavelength that identifies us, and the members in our pod do the same. If we want to find another member, we home in on their wavelength and follow it until we're in sight of each other. This sounds complex, but in reality it's quite simple and always accurate. We hope this answers your question.

We are thick-skinned

We are the Cetaceans and still able to swim through the oceans even with the ice and cold winds on the North Atlantic coast. Even though we are "thick-skinned" as you term it, we still feel the on-slaught of winter's ice and snowstorms.

There's no shelter out at sea, as we can't go close enough to mountain breakers on shore for protection from the winds. So while our physical bodies linger in the cold, our etheric bodies are "out and about" doing other tasks and feeling higher states of warmth and well-being which trickle down to the physical level, warming us from within. Thus, our etheric bodies and higher consciousness stabilizes and fortifies us in this cold air.

And you can do the same. You can call on your higher I AM Presence to warm, stabilize, and fortify your bodies on the cellular level, so the outer cold and chaos does not penetrate your physical shell. This way, you become oblivious to the extremes of temperatures and thoughts as you maneuver about on land.

Earth is a free will zone, which means that all who come here can choose their behavior and enact their roles on a grand scale. The test is to stand in your mighty I AM Presence and react to all around you from that place within you. Then nothing can shake or corrupt the purity of your soul. As you were thinking, we were "listening in," and understanding your thoughts concerning Earth as a free will zone. This is probably the greatest test, to remain solidly within your I AM Presence at all times, so that negativity can only bounce off you, while Love infiltrates your heart.

We in the oceans are always grounded in our mighty I AM Presence, and hence can go about our business unaffected by the catastrophes and chaos around us. For when in that higher frequency, all lower vibrations are out of sync and don't affect us. So we don't feel it, although we are still aware it exists and is happening on a lower plane.

We call out to you to capture the love and light being beamed to land from us out at sea. For this love and light is God's heart, opening to let you in.

Once you begin imbibing the mighty waves of love coming to you, **your heart will expand and DNA will reassemble itself,** all in the twinkling of an eye. You are mighty carriers of Light, beginning to remember who you are.

So this is our advice to you. Stay wrapped and in attunement with your Higher Self at all times, and know that nothing can touch you, except God's love as we Cetaceans experience it—and we experience it fully. We experience God's arms wrapped around us in a mighty embrace of love. We open our arms wide to enclose you in our embrace. We are your brothers and sisters out at sea.

All answers are encoded in your DNA

We are brave and courageous, and carry the keys to Earth's survival in our genes. We wish you to know that all the answers are encoded in your DNA strands, waiting for you to decode them as you climb into higher consciousness where you'll be able to access the storehouse of information that's within you. As you begin to access this information, you'll find that the keys to life will appear automatically each step of the way as you need them.

As you climb higher and higher on the path, you'll begin to be consciously aware of us and consciously in tune with our energy, so that you can tap into our consciousness at will, since we will soon be ONE consciousness climbing the path to greater and greater heights.

We are all connected as ONE, even now, although our energy is too faint for you to notice. But soon, as your consciousness increases, so too will the melody of our energy be brought to your ears as a symphony of Love from us to you.

Thank you for receiving this message. We are ONE with you all.

We monitor our brain waves
while awake and asleep

We are asleep and awake at the same time. We never really sleep—a part of us is always awake and alert while our other parts sleep—for fully sleeping in the oceans would be deadly, as you can imagine. We have our sonar system on fully, and it takes over while we snooze or sleep during the night.

When we're ready to awaken, a shift takes place in our consciousness and we switch from our full sonar alert system to our waking consciousness. This way, we are able to get in our required number of hours of sleep. Sounds like quite a feat, doesn't it? However, since we are fully conscious beings, it is quite easy and natural for us to make these transitory shifts.

Our brain waves also tell us what state we're in, and we're able to fully monitor our brain waves during our waking and sleeping hours. So we are fully alert mammals, even while sleeping. This gives us great latitude in our lives, and it is a great built-in protection device that we've strengthened over the many eons at sea.

Someday when you are all fully conscious, you, too, will be able to monitor yourself when you are sleeping, and then you can fully understand how this mechanism works for your protection.

Equipment for navigating the oceans is stored inside us

We are grouped together in this spring rain storm, waiting for the rain to stop. Spring is a wonderful time of year for us, a time of hope and rebirth for all life. It is our favorite time, as the temperatures are neither too hot nor too cold, but just perfect for our bodies' metabolism.

Our bodies are well equipped for our lives in the oceans. All the equipment we need for navigating the oceans is stored inside us, operating fully at optimal levels without the breakdowns you experience on land. Our tasks can all be accomplished with only our bodies. We need no other equipment to carry out our tasks for the Galactic Command. Everything we need is at our fingertips, so to speak, whereas you on land need many and sundry tools to accomplish your tasks and are dependent on them in order to succeed.

Take the computer for example. You need a big, bulky machine to make calculations for you, when all we need is our highly developed brain, which can compute five times faster than a computer. All the connections are "built-in" and our brains connect us to the universe's main computer system—the Source of ALL information.

We invite you to explore our thinking patterns by making a connection to our minds through your thoughts, for your thoughts can travel through the static of Earth and connect you to us. Then you will experience full consciousness again—your true and natural state of being.

Our lives run parallel to yours, even though we remain out at sea while you sit at desks all day. Swimming is certainly better for your back than sitting, and this is the one luxury we always have. There's certainly no need for us to see chiropractors! We are healthy, large, and strong, and our weight safely carries us along the currents as we wind our way through our vast food supply and millions of miles of waterways. We love you.

Our diet of plankton

Q: Don't you ever get tired of eating plankton every day? Do you ever miss foods such as chocolate cake with a cup of hot cappuccino?

A: We are the Cetaceans. We will answer your question. We have a varied diet, although you on the land may not think so. The foods we eat are rich in vitamins and nutrients, and give us the energy and strength we need to swim in the oceans. However, a hot cup of cappuccino may be pleasing to your palate, but not to ours. We eat only foods that invigorate us and that aid us in our work on Earth.

We have full consciousness, and we keep our consciousness clear by eating only those foods that enhance our clarity. We enjoy our food but not to the extent that we become addicted to certain food types as you do on land. We understand the reasons for eating certain foods and we are able to monitor our bodies to determine what we need.

When you move into full consciousness, you, too, will be able to monitor your bodily needs so that you can feed yourself specifically what you need each day. This way, you operate at optimum efficiency in all you think and do.

We send out blessings to you on the waves of the oceans, and as each wave rolls in, so do our blessings roll in to your shores, in anticipation of the day when there will be no fear of our coming to the shoreline to communicate and frolic with you again.

We thank you for posing this question to us. We are the Cetaceans, your brothers and sisters at sea.

We look for food while you shop for food

We go about our daily business, not unlike you. We look for food, while you shop for food. We eat all our meals raw, while you cook yours. We skip the preparation and clean-up, since there's nothing to prepare or clean. So in many ways, our eating habits free us from kitchen drudgery.

We keep all our utensils within our jaws. You, on the other hand, need many and sundry tools to prepare your food. As far as entertainment goes, we have a vast system of apparatus for our use. We can plug into any movie anywhere, or any book, and scan its pages in seconds, with full memory and understanding. So, we are at an advantage in this area, for all we need and want to know is at our finger tips, or "fin tips."

We can store vast amounts of information from whatever we choose to "watch" or "read." We are not limited to Earth for information, for we can consciously project to other planetary systems and scan their records. We can learn about many civilizations all over the universe because of our capacity to astral project to wherever we choose.

Someday soon, you, too, will be able to astral project your consciousness to far away places and bring back to your physical brain all the information you gathered.

So although our daily lives are different, once you attain full consciousness, this difference disappears, and you will be one with us in consciousness again.

Silica changes cells into light

We thrive in the oceans while you suffocate on land. The oceans supply us with all the oxygen we need to maintain our full consciousness and light bodies, while you on land are deprived of this vital source necessary for regeneration of your light bodies.

Oxygen is the key to the ascension! The more oxygenated foods you eat, the quicker you'll turn into light. Oxygen is found in all fresh organic fruits; and lettuce contains silica which changes your cells into light. So breathe deeply of fresh country air and drink fresh purified water, and you'll find your clarity of thought and peace again.

We in the oceans are very particular about our diet. We eat only fresh, "live" food and breathe deeply of the fresh ocean air. Our food and clean air keep us clear and strong and enable us to endure storms and other hardships without losing our strength or clarity of purpose.

You, on the other hand, are upset and confused over the simplest of life's problems, all because you've lost your balance and equilibrium due to your poor diet and inadequate supply of oxygen. Your body is a temple, needing only the highest source of food and air.

So treat yourselves as the kings and queens that you are, and feed your bodies only organic, fresh, live foods and note the difference. You'll feel lighter, swifter, and healthier as you increase your mutational pace into light.

We are the Cetaceans, and we beckon you to follow us as we merge headlong into light.

We are Great Beings of Light
carrying our Light to disseminate it on Earth.

We come from near and far,
and some of us have traveled great distances
to be here at this time.

We live by the seasons

We are the Cetaceans. We swim in your waters and bask in your sun. We enjoy each day for its own beauty. **We live in the NOW.** For us, there is no time, only the seasons of the year as they pass by. We live by the seasons, and our rituals and mating are seasonal displays of our instinctual ways of living.

You, too, live by instinct. You follow the seasonal changes by the way you adjust your life. You work during the winter months and vacation when it's warm. We do the same thing. We go about our life by bringing forth information that's relative to the seasons of time. For example, we fish for certain kinds of foods in the colder months when our main supply is short, and then return to certain places in the summer to renew our appetites for plankton and other varied delicacies.

We are also attuned to different frequencies in the colder months which help us keep warm. We raise our metabolic rate substantially in the summer and lower it during winter. These things you, too, will soon be able to do, as you rise in consciousness and take complete control of your bodies. For you, too, are multidimensional, and you, too, can raise and lower your metabolic rate as you choose. All multidimensional Beings can do this and more, as you'll soon find out when the Earth and all humanity rise into the fifth dimension and you wear your new body of Light.

So stay tuned to us, as together we rise in consciousness with all around us—as all life rises in tune to the same melody of Spirit. We are the Cetaceans, and we love you, our Sister on land.

Where are the Extinct Species of Cetaceans?

We are the Cetaceans who are extinct—or so you think. All species that are extinct are comprised of individuals whose souls are Immortal, thereby enabling them to reincarnate when the time is right. So we aren't lost or really "extinct," just our species' combined group frequency is, but we individuals remain alive in different bodies and on different planets in different dimensions.

We all look different each and every time we embody, but our souls always remain the same. We all come here to learn different experiences necessary for our soul growth, and leave after our lessons are learned, or when we are killed unexpectedly before we can complete our sojourn here.

It is no different now. You can ask yourselves the same questions, such as, "What was the Earth like when you were here thousands of years ago?" and, "Where are you now?"

Well, thousands of years ago many of you were also here on Earth in different bodies, when the Earth was still pristine and in balance and there was harmony. And where you are now is here again in a different body with a different face, and at a time when the Earth is in chaos and pain. We all recycle time and time again, to start anew again, hoping that "this time" we will complete our incarnational cycle and be able to move on.

The group presence of a specie generates a Light Field that is exponentially magnified by its members. It is this Light Field that is lost to Earth whenever a specie becomes extinct.

So only our species are extinct, but not the individuals who comprised them. And losing a specie is indeed a tragedy, for the wisdom and beauty of the group frequency they contributed to the Earth is irreplaceable. But we as individuals live on, just as you do now.

We use Astral Projection

The Cetaceans are here, swimming at this early hour of dawn when the fish are still slumbering and unaware of our presence as we glide quietly by. We love the Earth, we love humanity, and we love each other. Love is foremost in our lives and carries us through the water of life. It is our driving force and propels us through our days here, even as we yearn for our home back home. We know you yearn for your home in the higher dimensions too, and it is to these dimensions that we astral project when we are tired and weary and need an "Earth break," so to speak. It is better than coffee and gives us a boost without the caffeine. So we, too, have our ways of pumping adrenaline that is safe.

We congregate on the higher planes in our astral bodies and watch Earth from above. This gives us the vantage point of seeing all around us, and being able to use all we see when we return to our bodies under the sea where our range of vision is once again restricted.

Just as you use binoculars when viewing great distances, we use astral projection. It is cheaper and there is nothing to "carry." You already have all the "apparatus" you need to astral project. You only need to clear the pathway to access this "wonder" of travel, for it is built-in to the human species and meant to be used by all. It is this ability to travel "at will" that allows you to know all that exists, including your immortality. You then know All That Is through your own eyes, and this sight allows you to reach levels of understanding that have been thus far hidden from you. Sight is might. What you can reach, you can teach.

So reach to us in Love as we reach to you, and together we will help you reach out to the stars and bring back the information you need to understand the universe around you.

We are the Cetaceans and we love you.

Part Ten

Oceans

We call to you from the deepest parts
of the oceans.

We call to you from our hearts.

We call to you in songs sung
upon the ocean breezes.

There is no poverty or lack in the Oceans

We bring you news from the depths of the ocean *where all life is free*. We represent many classes of life forms, all living in the oceans and bays of Earth.

Our life is vastly different from yours, since we don't collect furnishings or material things for our environment. Instead, we live within the confines of our environment, using only what we need, when we need it. And of course our lifestyles are bountiful, and reflect the abundance that is all around us.

You, too, are surrounded by Earth's bountiful supply of resources. You need only to look around you at the vast array of abundance and then use only what you need. Your lives can be rich and diverse if you look to nature for your supply. *For nature supplies all life with everything it could possibly desire.*

We in the oceans realize this, and use nature to replenish our bounty when needed. There is no poverty or lack in the oceans, for we know that the Universe supplies all, and we live within the Divine Universal Laws and understand how to use our divinity and how to work within Universal Law.

You, too, can learn this way to live your life. Everything you need is at your disposal. *Just be aware of your divinity and connect yourself to the universal supply that exists all around you.* We are your brothers and sisters.

There is no poverty or lack in the oceans,

for we know that the universe supplies all.

Just be aware of your Divinity

and connect yourself to the universal supply

that exists all around you.

There's Genius in the Oceans

There's Genius in the Oceans
there's Wisdom in the Waves
slip inside my waters
and you shall find your way

Into our domain
it's very sane
no cargo ships
nor shipping lanes

It's safe to Swim
on just a whim
for our domain
exists on a higher plane

That's free from humans
pollution too
we just glide along
and sing our songs

So come with us
our vibration's high
and you shall reach
the other side

Where all is Love
all is Light
where all in Heaven
know our plight

We reach to you
we sing to you
to help us now
as we bring you through

The gates to Heaven
are opening wide
just merge with us
we'll take you inside

To our domain
where we will remain
until all on Earth
reach a Higher Plane

Then we will merge
as One Light from above
and sail the Seas
on the wings of the dove

We'll swim and glide
as we merrily ride
across the Seas
on Freedom's tide

FREEDOM
it's waiting for us all
so open your ears
and hear our call

Merge your Light

with ours in the oceans.

Begin now by focusing your intent on us,

and we will connect with you from our end,

into one glorious connection of LIGHT.

Water is just another school

Greetings from Earth's oceans! We greet you in the name of the *one Creator* of all life, in and out of water. For water is just another school where other species live, play, and learn Earth lessons, as you do on land.

Our earthly lessons follow the same curriculum as yours does. We set goals and then go about achieving them according to our ways, and tuning into our guidance systems just as you do on land.

We also have guides and guardian angels who work directly with us in the oceans, for there are no barriers to God's guidance, and all are given the opportunity to follow their hearts and develop their intuitive capacity to reach higher and higher into the *All That Is*. And *All That Is is One*, one Source for all, no matter what delineation the species appears to be in the third dimension of illusion. We are all *one* in the higher dimension of Love and Light.

So swim with us in the stream of life, where our thoughts converge in one mighty ocean of light.

The Oceans are never clear anymore

I am a Sperm Whale. We're swimming off the coast of Nova Scotia, and thank you for connecting with us today. Our family is small, and what's left of us mostly swim alone in trepidation of trawlers and other destructive devices that are strewn in our way.

The oceans are never clear anymore, and swimming is risky these days, not like the past when we were free to swim without fear of being killed or mangled. It would be as if you walked outside your house and had to tiptoe for fear of stepping on explosives or being run over by a cement truck. We wait patiently for the Ascension to occur and carry us back home.

Come and swim with us
in your dream time,
and know these waters will be safe.
For your dreams are
in a higher dimension,
where all is protected.

There is nothing we lack
except safe seas in which to swim

We are the Cetaceans, calling to you from the depths of the oceans. Our voices sing to you on the waves of the sea. Our love for you flows from our hearts, and races toward you to receive. We are ever broadcasting our love for you over the waves of the sea. Someday soon we hope to join you on land as one species joins another in love and respect and hope for our combined future on Earth.

We love Earth. It is our home away from home. And although we miss our home planet, we are grateful to the Earth for all she has given us. *We are perfectly blessed with abundance on every level. There is nothing we lack, except, of course, safe seas in which to swim.*

Mother Earth has given us this, but man, in his greed, has made our home unsafe to move around in. Soon this will change, for greed will not be part of the fifth dimension. Those in greed will stay behind and continue their wanton ways on another third dimensional planet. We will then have our home back, and we will be free to wander from coast to coast without harm and in full protection of the one Creator.

So come and swim with us in your dream time, and know these waters will be safe, for your dreams are in a higher dimension where all is protected.

We are the Cetaceans and we love you.

We swim with humans who are lost at sea

We are the Cetaceans. We are grouped together as we broadcast this message to you. We swim in the seas and bask in the sun. We are friendly and jovial, and welcome all humans who enter our waters. *For the oceans are for all, just as your land is for all.* No one is barred from entering our oceans. We often swim with the humans who are floundering out at sea, until help arrives or until we can guide them to shore.

We take great pride in our prowess and strength, and great responsibility when someone is lost out at sea. Many times we are able to telepathically contact humans who are adrift and give them information that will guide them back to land.

There are so many ways that we could work with you, if you would but recognize us as equal to you. That is the way it was supposed to be originally, when the Earth was populated with so many different species. We all had our own roles to play, and we all had our roles to play with each other.

This was the perfect plan, had humans not deviated from it. It was the Divine Plan that would have led us all in a much different direction than we now find ourselves. We could have reached the summit of glory long ago, instead of reaching the bottom of degradation in which we now find our Earth.

So let's begin now and enter into a partnership that will bring us and all Earth to greater heights of understanding and greater heights of glory than we now find ourselves in. **It is not too late.** We await your call, and will work with you at night in your dream state.

Farewell, our brothers and sisters on land.

We are friendly and jovial,
and welcome all humans who enter our waters.
For the oceans are for all,
just as your land is for all.

We Whales Patrol the Shorelines

Mikey is here. I am swimming in the murky waters off Delaware, looking for my morning breakfast of shrimp and herring and cod. There isn't too much life close to the coast, as we can't breathe near the shore.

As a rule, we all stay as far from shore as possible, so as not to get entangled in fishing lines and tuna nets. However, the smaller fish swarm toward the shore, as they like to rest in the nooks and crannies jutting out from the coastline. We Whales patrol the shoreline and often come in close for a better view. But as for our breakfast, the fish farther out in the Ocean are healthier to eat. So we will wait awhile for breakfast, then swim out farther.

Life in the Oceans is busy these days—as our home is being invaded by people, ships, and underwater experiments. We've no privacy left anymore, and must separate ourselves to survive. The farther apart we stay from each other, the safer it is, as we're less likely to be seen or noticed from a distance if there's only one of us.

So after my breakfast, I'll return for patrol duty along the northeast coast, where I radio back information to the Galactic Command in response to the inquiries regarding matters of environmental concerns and safety.

The early morning hours are the most precious and invigorating for us, as the Life Force is flowing freely through to the Earth, unencumbered by humanity's thought-waves and concerns. The heaviness of your thoughts and cares weighs down and deadens the Life Force until it is only a trickle, barely enough to sustain Life, which is why humans die so young and are so weak—they shut out the Life Force necessary to sustain them.

So, everything is working against you, and you have created it all yourself. You have blocked yourself off from receiving the Life sustaining forces from the Universe. You, yourselves, have shortened your life spans to mere decades instead of centuries — all through your thoughts, rape of the land, and lack of reverence for Life.

You all came to Earth to care for her and flourish, but instead you end your life by destroying her and yourself at an early age. You got lost on your incarnational journey, and can't get back through the mire and decay of your errant lifestyles and distorted thoughts. So you flounder through your lives until they unglamorously end in pain and sorrow and regret.

This time there will be no repeat performance, as humanity is off the wheel of Karma and back on the spiral of evolution. So you either have to want to evolve or will be returned to another third dimensional planet for a repeat performance. The choice is yours. But one thing is certain, and that is that Life goes on — with or without Earth humans.

So spend your day in communion with us — listen to the waves roll into your heart and feel our presence surrounding you and our love caressing your skin. Maintain conscious contact with us and we will guide you safely through Earth's passage to the stars.

I am Mikey — ever vigilant, patrolling your shores.

Use Other Means to Transport Your Cargo

It is I, Mikey the Whale. The Sea is choppy tonight as big cargo freighters are carrying goods through our passageways and churning up the waves. But we don't mind, as these ships are benign and don't harm us. As long as we avoid their paths there are no collisions.

We do avoid them when we can see them near us, but if we should surface too quickly without looking up, then we could find ourselves beneath them. This is as if you go on a walk or run and expect the path ahead to be free of debris and blockages and then reach the end and you're smack into a wall — seemingly from nowhere.

The Ocean is our pathway, and we don't like it encumbered by fishing vessels, cargo ships, or whaling boats. After all, this is our home we are talking about. Our home is our sanctuary, just as your home is your sanctuary.

When you walk into a room in your house, you wouldn't want to find it inhabited by a boat or ship—would you? Well, the different parts of the ocean are our rooms too, so to speak, and when we enter them we want them to be free of intruders, just as you would want your rooms to be free of intruders. Surely, there are other ways to travel and to ship goods and commodities.

Follow the model used in the Subterranean Cities, where they use their electromagnetic rail system to transport commodities, or the Hollow Earth, where they also use their electromagnetic trains instead of putting shipping vessels in their oceans. In the Inner Earth they don't disrupt the Sea People in their homes under the sea. On the contrary, they respect and honor their presence, as they respect and honor all people, whether they are residing on land or in the seas.

So this is our message to you today: It is for Earth Humans to use other means to transport their cargo so that the Seas can be freed for our use—as we can't live on land or in the air. The Oceans are our only home. So please leave "our" property and stop trespassing into our zone, which belongs to our life form—just as we don't trespass on your land.

We let you live in peace. All we ask is that you let us live in peace. We are all One Soul living on different parts of Earth. Please respect our existence, as we respect yours.

Why Do You Trespass on Our Property?

I am Mikey swimming out at Sea—FREE—in the mid to southern Atlantic Ocean, where all is in green and with blue sky surrounding our domain. Our domain is our property zone, just as your domain is the landforms surrounded by the Oceans.

The Oceans are our home and the land is yours. So why do you trespass on our property? The Earth is large enough for all forms of life to have their own habitats without infringing on the others. When you move into another specie's habitat, you destroy the environment that is crucial for that life form to survive and live in a balanced existence. You upset nature and unbalance the ecology, so that neither the encroached upon nor the encroacher benefits.

The Earth was perfectly balanced until mankind lost their connection with Source. All was in abundance and peace and harmony until mankind "thought" that the Earth was theirs to own and mine and strip and rape and pillage and kill and mutilate for their own amusement and greed.

It takes a planet billions and trillions of years to develop Earth's environment into a perfect home that provides everything that everyone could possibly need and want for all species, and yet mankind goes on its blind way, killing and mutilating all in its path and making excuses and giving reasons to justify its destruction of the Earth—as if anything could justify the killing of a planet.

We in the Oceans have reached our limit of tolerance after all these thousands of years of torture and torment to our families and friends. We use the term "mankind" here, because it has been the male energy of aggression that has been primarily responsible for Earth's destruction and imbalance. All life forms have been in balance and working toward balancing and rebalancing Earth in the wake of humanity's desolation.

Oceans of waste

We are the Cetaceans. We dive deep in the oceans. We find things in the oceans that were buried millions of years ago. These things don't biodegrade. They retain their shape for eons. It is up to humanity to dispose of their goods in better ways—ways that do not leave the debris of waste.

The time will come when the oceans will be full of waste materials and we won't have a natural habitat of our own. When this happens, all of the Earth will suffer the consequences of its wastefulness. *For without water there cannot be life.* And without life, there cannot be humans.

So you can only benefit from your vigilance, and prosper from taking care of your waste materials in ways that do not injure the Earth. For all life has waste, and yet all life disposes of its waste in discreet ways that do not clog the arteries and heart of Mother Earth.

The Earth is a most beautiful place to incarnate, and from outer space, the Earth is astounding! Some day when you have the technology to travel in space, you will see the grandeur of the planet you live and breathe on.

Mother Earth only wishes the very best of living conditions for you and your children, and your part is to use only what you need, and to recycle everything in such a way that it filters back into the land and water in ways that utilize its life force and productivity to meld back into nature to be reused again and again.

Other civilizations have wasted and squandered the Earth's resources, and their fate was similar to the conditions you now see prevalent on Earth. They ran out of clean drinking water and clean air, and suffocated in their own generated filth.

However, we are all here trying to prevent the same fate from occurring again, and to bring your consciousness level up to heights where you can remedy Earth's plight before it's too late. We are all here to help you, if you will *just take time out of your busy day to hear us and listen to the Earth herself.* For she is constantly sending you messages, too. Remember, it's never too late, especially with all the Light that's now on Earth.

We drink a toast to you with a gulp of clean ocean water, still pure and still sparkling clear. We are the Cetaceans and we love you.

Pollution destroying Earth's body

We live in your oceans safe from your pollution. We find our life easy and joyous, for the farther out we swim from your shores, the easier it is to breathe the air. We await the time when all Earth is cleaned from the pollution that is destroying her body. For Earth has a glorious body of beauty, with streams and rivers as her heartline and mountains and meadows as her nerve centers.

We await the time when you on land will awaken to the Earth's beauty and treat her with the respect and care she so deserves. Until that time, we continue to bathe you in our Light and to send you our Love from afar.

Polar ice caps melting

Know that your rivers and lakes swell over due to the melting of the polar caps. You will find many places inundated by water from rivers and lakes. As your water supply reserve increases, know that there will be imbalances in your weather system, for this melting is NOT natural. **It is due to the air pollution caused by humanity and the destruction of the planet's rain forests.**

We in the oceans will be affected by this imbalance also, as our water supply increases in depth and changes the contour of the land. This affects all life on land and in the sea. A balanced ecology is most imperative to healthy specie survival, no matter where their habitat. We all need clean water, clean air, and a natural environment that is healthy and balanced. These factors are lacking today. In fact, everything is out of balance and affecting everything else.

As you rise in frequency, your awareness of planetary life will increase, and you will begin to know how to remedy and rebalance the elements on Earth. So your awakening and evolution is critical to the planet. *For you can change the pattern, thereby changing the future from one of disaster to one of balance and harmony.*

We invite you to study with us in your dream state, and attend our nightly sessions which are held on the inner planes in your etheric states. We all come together and learn, play, and reconnect to the One Light Source where all the answers are. So come and play with us at night, while we all plan for our Earth's emergence into Light.

We are your brothers and sisters.

Response to
"Earthquakes take place in oceans"

Q: In response to the Earth changes, there are those who make affirmations that "all earthquakes take place in the oceans so as to cause minimal, or no, loss of life."

A: We are the Cetaceans, living deep in your oceans, and replying to this statement. Whose lives are they talking about here?

Know that there's life in your oceans! We, who are in full consciousness, live in the oceans and the oceans are our home. There are hundreds of millions of other life forms inhabiting the oceans also, with a complete ecosystem that is healthy and balanced and in tune with Earth. Do you really want to say affirmations that will destroy our home with earthquakes just because you have destroyed yours with errant thought patterns and pollution?

Think again before you bring doom to the oceans with your thoughts. Earthquakes under the oceans would cause mass flooding on the coastlines and destroy *your* lives as well as ours. Why destroy our lives when you are the ones responsible for all the chaos and confusion on land?

The Earth changes are in direct response to humanity's negativity, carelessness, greed, rape of the land, and pollution of the air. Why must we, in the oceans, suffer the consequences for what you, on land, have created?

Please be aware of all the other life forms in existence, before you "think" us into non-existence.

We are the Cetaceans, and *the oceans are our home*.

Weather Anomalies are Unnatural

Mikey is here, waiting for you out at Sea, where I pick up your frequency range. Know that I wait for you every morning, hoping you will pick up my signal and reply to my call. Today we will talk about rain — the floods and quakes and tornadoes on land.

El Nino is just a guise to cover up underwater testing experiments that are being done under the ground and in the Oceans. The governments are themselves disrupting the weather patterns by their testing devices and explosives that destroy the eco-balance of the Earth's atmosphere and biosphere, causing anomalies and disruptions in Nature.

Nature is in balance and harmony and peacefulness when left alone and not tampered with. It is only man's hands that disrupt the landscape and seascape, causing mass flooding and winds. Their testing has caused the jet stream to move off its normal path, thus disrupting the whole atmospheric layer of Earth.

Your secret government is using experimental devices to destroy Life on this planet and poison humans to decrease the world's population so that they can better control the few humans that will be left. This is their intention, and the confusion and chaos is a part of their plan.

We in the Oceans are being directly affected too, as their devices are deadly when magnified in intensity by the water element. The sounds become so loud under water that they vibrate at rates that cause pain and confusion to all Sea Life. The only escape from these torturous devices is to beach our selves or go insane.

Flooding and hurricanes and tornadoes and earthquakes are not natural and certainly don't occur in the Inner Earth or in the Subterranean cities. So you must question, why are these calamities occurring on the Earth's surface? They are occurring because your governments are causing them to occur — all to control Earth's population and resources so that a very few can own all the planet and all the wealth. This is a travesty of Justice and of Divine Law, and these covert groups won't be allowed to succeed in their plan but will be removed to another third dimensional planet.

Earth is extremely well monitored by the Galactic Command and Beings from other Star Systems who know precisely what occurs and by whom. We are not in the dark as you Earth humans are—we are cognizant of all that transpires.

So don't think your weather anomalies are natural—the only natural factors are peace and balance and harmony. When you are in peace and balance and harmony, you are in your natural state. Everything else is out of Nature or unnatural. The same for the Earth—her natural state is out of balance, reflecting the imbalance of humans and their destructive technology.

So stop waging war against the Earth and against each other. We have all done our part, and now it's up to you. You can either live in peace or be mind controlled and enslaved by your nefarious governments. The choice is yours.

I am Mikey, out at Sea.

HAARP* and erratic weather

We bask in the sun this time of year, although the weather conditions are erratic, with long lapses of sunshine. When it is colder, we huddle together offshore, waiting for the warm air from land to drift over us. We love our life out at sea, and if it weren't for erratic weather conditions caused by HAARP and other government experiments, we'd be lazily basking in the noonday sun instead of huddled up from the cold and rain, waiting for the sun to shine.

Which brings us to the subject of this communication: life on Earth. Know that in order for life to exist in harmony and balance, **humans must learn the laws of nature and abide by their laws.** This way the Earth and all life will flow balanced into one another in consciousness and love. Erratic patterns only cause separation, distance, and disharmony, while stability and balance lead to evolution. **Someday soon you will know just how much your lives and weather patterns are interfered with, limiting your evolution in ways that will surprise you. For limitation of any kind impedes progress of a species and jeopardizes evolution.**

We in the seas know all this through our observation of the land, as we lie at rest in the oceans, monitoring your land masses. When you all rise in consciousness, you will find yourselves in the Earth's comfort zone once again. We thank you for communicating with us.

* HAARP (High-frequency Active Auroral Research Project) has been designed to beam more than 1.7 gigawatts (billion watts) of radiated power into the ionosphere, the electrically charged layer above the Earth's atmosphere. It will "boil the upper atmosphere," after which the radiation will bounce back onto Earth in the form of long waves which will penetrate our bodies, the ground, and the oceans. (Excerpted from Angels Don't Play This Haarp, from the foreword by·Dr. Gael Crystal Flanagan and Dr. Patrick Flanagan)

Part Eleven

Galactic Connections

We have come from
many different Star Systems
to help Earth in her climb into light.

We are totally connected to the Galactic Federation of Planets

Greetings from Earth's oceans. We are assembled around you, listening to your thought waves as they are generated from your brain and flow out to us on the ethers of Earth's oceans. We are the Earth's Cetaceans, floating on the waves of the sea, listening and waiting for your calls to come to us. We wait and long to reply to your questions about Earth, the Galactic Command, and the Photon Belt. Thank you for your questions. We will answer them from our one group mind consciousness, flowing out to you from all of us, in and out of embodiment.

We sing to you of Earth, the golden goddess of Light, floating majestically through the universe on her course through the stars. We are all her travelers, sitting on her body as she majestically carries us through the starry skies. We are on a golden disc that is alive and conscious of all life passing by. We are golden light, densified by matter, moving up and out of third dimensional consciousness.

We are not alone on Mother Earth, although to your five senses, it appears so. Rather, we are totally connected to the Galactic Federation of Planets, which oversees our galaxy and this sector of the universe. The Galactic Federation has always worked with Cetaceans, in tandem with our Earth mission. It is through the Federation that we are able to receive the information we need in order to carry through our multi-level tasks on behalf of our Earth Mother.

The Federation and we are ONE. We work together, always, on many different levels, always representing the Earth and humanity's highest intentions. Ascension is first and foremost in our minds, and we always keep these thoughts focused as a strong beam guiding us through the waters of life.

Know that all life on Earth is aware of the Ascension process through which we are moving, and that all life is ascending continually, even as we speak. It is a process that, once put into motion, only accelerates in speed, until one day you will all wake up seeing us stand before you encased in golden light, and welcoming you back again to the waters of flowing light.

We all wait for you to wake up to the Light Beings that you are, and to see us through your third eye once again—the eye of inner vision where all of existence is exposed. You are all very dear to us, all of humanity in all its different levels of consciousness. For these levels are just growth levels, and someday all of you will all be with us together in consciousness again.

For this game we all are playing is soon to come to an end, and we will all regroup and evaluate our various roles and parts in the great drama called life. Then we will all continue on a higher frequency, on the next step of consciousness, in our ever spiraling journey through eternity. We all just keep moving closer and closer to God, playing different parts, as we individually and as a group learn our lessons of co-creatorship and mastery of ourselves on all levels, until we reach the next plateau.

The Galactic Federation serves as our guide, and gives us the loving support and technical help we need to complete our mission on Earth. Without their knowledge and foresight, we would be lost in the density of the Earth plane, and we would not be able to carry out our tasks that are so vital to our existence and to the existence of all life on Earth.

We bathe in the glory of Light that is showered to us from above, and that keeps us balanced and attuned to God's purpose, while we swim through the chaos of the murky waves of humanity's thoughts.

So come and swim with us—as we swim with you—and know that you will all, someday soon, be free to swim with us in your thoughts. We love you, our dear sisters and brothers, and we hope to be with you soon in total consciousness.

We breathe with you as *one*.

Our work with the Galactic Command

Today it is rainy out at sea. There is a storm brewing on the horizon. We defer our tasks until the sea is calmer. There is so much to do out in the oceans, that sometimes we must postpone our work as you do on land.

Our work is simple. **We work directly with the Galactic Command for this sector of the galaxy.** We do a lot of "sightseeing," as you might say, although our work involves a lot of detail that is necessary for thoroughly reporting what we find. We look for anything unnatural either in the water or on land in the coastal areas. We look for devices that may be planted at sea that are harmful to both humans and to us. We can see the landforms off the coastal waters, and can detect any foreign objects. This helps the Galactic Command monitor the territory in question and to remove or defuse these deadly devices.

So our jobs aren't that pleasant, and yet they are very important, for we are still the **Guardians of Earth** and still responsible for its care and safety. We look forward to the time when all species will live in peace, and this kind of vigilance is unnecessary. **We look forward to the time when you will resume your job as stewards and caretakers of Earth.**

We came from different Star Systems

My Dear Child of the Earth: We are the Cetaceans, greeting you from beneath the waters of your oceans. We are here with you on Earth's journey to the stars. We are here in great numbers, preparing for the Earth's emergence into Light.

We came here especially for this time when the Earth is in transit to a higher dimension. We are here in our full consciousness, waiting patiently for Earth's children to bloom into the Caretakers you were meant to be. We have been brought to Earth from different star systems, just as you have, as all of us have, to bring the Earth through her ascension on the other side of the veil.

We are here in vast numbers monitoring your Earth and skies by using our sonar to pick up deadly and destructive devices that could harm Earth's children on land and in the sea. We have the vast capability of detecting those devices that are out of sync with the natural surroundings of Earth. We use this gift of detection to report our findings to the Galactic Command, which in turn investigates our sightings.

Communicating with Galactic Command

We are the Cetaceans. Today it is sunny and the ocean waves are high. We can see far to the horizon just beyond the sky. The waves lap up on the shore, bringing in the small ocean fish and seaweed. It is beautiful today.

We reach to each other using our high frequencies of sound that penetrate the water. We all gather together at this time, and stay in groups for safety. At night, we take turns keeping watch while our pods sleep.

Life is exciting for us, since we are able to contact and communicate with the Galactic Command for this sector of the galaxy. They could even beam us aboard ship, but we are a little too big to really fit; so we go on board with our consciousness instead, and stay as long as we like. With our full consciousness, we can be in two places at once.

Freedom of Passage

We are here, not far off the coast, frolicking in the mid-morning sun and floating on the waves. Today the current is strong, buoying our bodies to and fro in the wind. We sing and play with each other after a large breakfast of shrimp and herring—one of our favorites. We eat huge amounts of foods that we rapidly digest due to our constant movement of swimming, racing, diving, and breaching. We burn up the calories as soon as we consume them. There's no extra fat on us. We are as sleek as a deer and strong as an ox.

We are continually exercising as we go about our day's work for the Galactic Command, showing them the areas that need patrolling in order to protect the Earth from those intent on transgressing it. We are carefree, yet diligent in our work, always carefully scouting the oceans and land masses in our vicinity, and then reporting our findings to the Galactic Command for this sector of our galaxy.

There is always so much to do, and not enough of us to do it. So we work quickly, leaving plenty of time to still be with our families and pods.

Many Cetaceans are leaving the Earth plane due to its density and pollution, and the wanton killing of our lives. It is no longer the haven we once frolicked in, and our lives are in daily danger from those who track us down. Our lives would be so easy, if only mankind would stop and listen, and learn how to live within the Universal Laws where he will find the peacefulness and abundance he yearns for. "Stop and listen" is our motto. It is a way out of your self-inflicted chaos that you've created out of greed and ego. There is no greed in the oceans: All is shared and all is in abundance.

No one owns anything, and yet all is owned by everyone. All is the gift of the *one* Creator — the Creator of life in and out of the oceans. For all life comes from the same source, no matter what its form or level of consciousness. And we in the oceans love our forms and delight in our consciousness. For we are fully evolved Beings inhabiting our ocean bodies for expediency and delight — the delight of floating and navigating the Earth freely without constraint or the necessity of obtaining passports or licenses. In fact, the freedom from paperwork and the freedom from having to purchase our passage through the oceans with money is the greatest freedom of all. We come and go when we please, without having to save up money for our trips. This free passage unites our species and brings us all closer together as one family.

There are no restraints to separate us in the oceans. **Your separateness is your government's desire to keep you all isolated in order to better control you. Without freedom of passage, your intimacy and knowledge of one another is minimal, and your differences magnified, causing distrust and wars.**

So come together in extended families as we do, and you will delight in the safety and security of life. We are the Cetaceans and we love you.

We monitor the oceans

We are the Cetaceans living deep within the oceans of the Earth plane. Many of us have chosen to leave this planet because of the perils we face each day. Yet many of us remain as the Guardians of this Earth. Without us, there would be no-one to monitor the oceans, and the Confederation would be without our guidance.

We make many discoveries daily in our journey through the waters that help remedy and stabilize the grids surrounding the planet. There is much adjustment going on daily to keep your planet from wobbling on its course through the stars.

We, in the oceans, are in the unique position of reporting atmospheric conditions to the Confederation. We relay great amounts of atmospheric information to Mission Control to correct Earth's wobble and axis alignment.

These are the things that make our life and work here interesting. We're part of the Great Mind of the Creator, and our job is to report conditions that interfere with the workings and mechanisms of the unique grid system of Earth. As long as we are here, we will continue to report our findings to Mission Control, until the time when you, as Caretakers of Earth, will be able to continue on your own. Until that time, we will remain here en masse, even though some of us will continue to leave for our home planet.

We have mapped out
the bottom of the oceans

We dive in the oceans as a form of delight and play. We hunt for coral and gemstones along the banks and bottoms of water. We find a wealth of interesting artifacts intact on the bottom of the oceans that divers have attempted to recover but with little success, since they have no way of determining their precise location. However, we have "mapped out" the bottom of the oceans, since the ocean floors are unsafe and laden with rusted and dangerous mines and objects that cut and scrape our skin. We know where each artifact, gemstone, and munition lies. This is our job, and we store this information in our ancient memory banks for the time when we can relay it directly to you—for the time when we will all be united as *one*.

We also have the land mapped out, showing where nuclear devices are and where ground surfaces are not safe due to buried landmines, radiation, and pollution. We expect our planet to do all she can to protect herself by ridding herself of these pollutants through any way she deems appropriate. She has cared long enough for humanity without humanity returning the caring. For Mother Earth to be safe, she must be able to feel clear water flowing through her veins.

We used to be able to swim through our oceans unharmed, just as you walk through your streets unharmed, knowing that you won't be endangered by stepping on mines or other dangerous devices along your path. We are receiving aid from the Galactic Command, and yet they cannot clear the ocean bottoms until they can land and are given approval from the Spiritual Hierarchy who are overseeing the Earth operation. So we wait and endure, and hope that Earth's children learn to respect our home in the sea as we respect your home on land.

Mines on the ocean floor

Today we will talk about the mines that are found on the bottom of the oceans. Know that there are obsolete munition dumps on the floors of our oceans. Although these weapons are now defunct, still they exude dangerous chemicals and litter our oceans.

The ocean is our habitat, and we don't like our "floors" to be cluttered with dangerous weapons, chemicals, and metals. Just as you on land like the freedom to walk in your homes, so do we like to be able to sink to the ocean's bottom and rest there if we wish.

So when the Confederation lands as Earth enters the Photon Belt, one of the first tasks will be a cleanup of our ocean floors. We will oversee this operation, guiding the work crews to specific locations for dematerialization of this clutter.

We work alongside the Confederation in many areas and in many ways. Although our bodies remain in the seas, our consciousness goes wherever we direct our thoughts. For we are multidimensional, and while we swim in Earth's oceans, we are on assignment in other dimensions simultaneously. We can be in two places at once, and often are.

So swim with us during your dream time, and we will show you the wonders of the sea.

The ocean floors are unsafe
and laden with rusted and dangerous mines
and objects that cut and scrape our skin.

Q: Why can't you see the fishing nets and whaling ships so that you can avoid them?

A: Know that it is very dark in the sea and we oftentimes miss the very objects that we are reporting. We can scan the horizon and usually see them, but sometimes we are distracted by our other tasks or concerns and don't see them. Then we find ourselves dead-ended in the obstacle that we might have sighted only days before. We know this sounds curious to you, but it happens. Just as if you're driving down a busy street full of repairs and note some obstacle, and then the next day you drive right into it because your mind is on something else. So it happens to us too.

As to the Galactic Command for this sector of the galaxy, they would like to dematerialize the fishing nets and harpoons and other deadly weapons used to entrap and kill us, but then they would be directly interfering in the lives of another planet. Universal Law does not allow them this sanction, and they must watch helplessly as we fall prey to these whaling tactics.

In order for a planet to receive help from off-planet, the people must ask for intervention in their lives. It is only through the Law of Asking that you receive. The Asking must come from the humans themselves, as we have volunteered to be here to help you evolve on the ladder of consciousness.

If we asked for direct intervention on our behalf, then the lessons that humanity needs to learn would become non-existent. We are your teachers, yet you are destroying the very ones who came here to save you from yourselves.

Petition the Spiritual Hierarchy of Earth to intervene on behalf of all Cetaceans

Know that we long for peace in the oceans, as you long for peace on Earth. We have come from many different star systems to help Earth in her climb into light. We were here in great numbers, although now our numbers have rapidly dwindled. We welcome your coming to our aid to petition the Spiritual Hierarchy of Earth to intervene on behalf of all your brothers and sisters out at sea.

We welcome direct intervention, after all these millennia of non-intervention. We strive to do all that we can to help this sweet Earth, and yet we cannot do it all by ourselves. We, as divine consciousness, must work together from all levels and all dimensions to bring more Light into the Earth. **This way, people will realize how interconnected all species are and whaling would become non-existent overnight.**

We meet with the Spiritual Hierarchy and describe our plight and the plight of humans who are at the mercy of the dark forces, too. Yes, there is the law of non-interference, and yet there is much interference going on from levels of which humans are not yet aware.

We advise you to work closely with us in spirit, so that our combined consciousness can overcome the darkness that is prevalent on Earth. We welcome the direct intervention of the Confederation on our behalf, and we, too, feel that it is time for action — time for the Light to prevail and dispel the darkness.

We will meet with you on the Inner Planes of Light and Love, and support your plea to the Spiritual Hierarchy on our behalf. Although we are patient and peaceful, we, too, feel that it is time for action, as we don't want to see our stock further decimated out of greed and ignorance.

Thank you for coming to our aid and for speaking out on our behalf. **We are all in this together — all life on Earth — and bringing** our cause to the direct attention of all members of the Spiritual Hierarchy will make very clear the odds we face here on Earth, and how their intervention is so vitally necessary to our cause.

We trust your actions and know that you work tirelessly for us on the Outer and Inner Planes. Soon peace will reign on Earth and we will look back on this in wonderment and joy for all we have accomplished. We are your brothers and sisters out at sea.

Repairing the Earth's Magnetic Grid

We are the Cetaceans, greeting you on this fine day in July. The weather is calm, warm, and balmy, and the ocean breezes stir the waves as they rise and fall in unison with the Earth's magnetic pull.

Life in the oceans is exciting. There is always something to do, no matter how we're feeling or what we're thinking, for we are in touch with many different places at the same time. We keep track of the many different locations where the Earth's magnetic grid is weakened and in need of repair, and where the Confederation is trying to strengthen it.

We work in unison with all who are here as conscious caretakers, in order to correct and rectify Earth's etheric and physical structure. There is so much that has been destroyed and weakened through humanity's misuse and carelessness, that on some days it seems this is all we do.

For example, today we reported a missing link in part of Earth's magnetic structure that was lost due to the huge amount of air pollution and negativity filtering through the Earth's etheric encasement. The Earth is encased in a shield because of the danger of her polluted body spreading out in space, and it is this dangerous level of toxins to which we're constantly alert. We report problems to the Galactic Command, which uses its technology to dematerialize whatever pollution they can. This is quite a job, but one we easily handle.

We are the Record Keepers of the planet

We are here. Yes, we follow your time periods in the oceans. We have time demarcations that fully utilize your time frame on the land. We report directly to the Galactic Command in regular intervals of your time. We keep records of all vital information in our memory banks and give this information out to the Galactic Command when asked. Thus, we are able to store large amounts of information at a time. We are ever ready to use our large memory banks for the good of the Earth.

We are the Record Keepers of the planet. We have kept and stored all Earth's history in our memories, which are available to tap when the time for their release is at hand. All of Earth's children will be given this information when it's time.

Our time is the same as your time on land, although we keep track of the days and years differently than you do. Our days and years follow the stars overhead. We can tell what time frame we're in by looking at the night sky, which clearly marks the passage of time for us.

We are the Earth Keepers

We are the Cetaceans. We are the great Record Keepers on Earth. We keep records on all Earth activity in the oceans and on the land. We are vigilant. We watch your water and your skies, and we know if anyone transgresses Earth's code of ethics in regard to humanity as established by the Galactic Command. If so, we immediately contact the Galactic Command and report our findings.

We are not only the Earth's record keepers, but also the Earth Keepers. We love the Earth. We love all humanity, and wait patiently for all of humanity to recognize us as their equals and respect us as their elders.

We bring you love from the oceans surrounding your land. We sing to you of ancient times when we all lived together as one on the Earth. Those times will return when we, once again, visit you on land.

We were once living our lives on land, long, long ago. We had to leave our homes on land and move into the oceans to survive. Now with all the Earth and planetary changes and planetary Light, we will once again feel safe on land.

We long for that time when we can safely swim or safely bask in the sun without being alert for danger. This will give us great latitude in our activities and allow us the pleasure of relaxing our vigil.

We can easily adapt to land again, and become the creatures we once were. We won't feel so confined to the oceans, and will be able to come close to you on shore. *The time is soon coming when we will merge our minds from the oceans with your minds on shore, as ONE MIND.*

We love you, our Sister on shore.

One Group Mind

The Cetaceans are here. We send you greetings from the Earth's oceans. We are *one group mind*, broadcasting our thoughts to you from the depths of the oceans. We cast our nets of thoughts out to you, so to speak, to hold you in our consciousness.

We are ever hoping to connect more and more with Earth humans in hope of creating an alliance with your species that will protect our lives on the seas.

We are here in great numbers monitoring your oceans. We track all movements in the Earth's depth and relay our information to the Galactic Command. We are the Guardians of the Earth, and have taken over your role of stewardship until you can again resume it. We, too, will be making the transition into Light, and we will be guiding you through the Photon Belt.

Our thoughts are always going out to you on the waves of the oceans. We are always waiting and ready to connect with you on land. Although we are confined to the water, our thoughts travel out to the universe and carry our feelings and information to all who connect to our wavelength.

We are so joyous to be connected to you on land. **You can now convey our thoughts through this book, where we will have an outlet at last.** We thank you for connecting with us, and for being our spokesperson at this time of Earth changes.

Stay tuned to our frequency, as we are attuned to yours. **We *salute you in the light.***

The Cetaceans

We crave our home planet

We are the Cetaceans. We inhabit your seas and we dwell there in peace. We come together at certain times to rest and recover from our arduous journeys through the oceans. Many of us fall prey to fishing vessels. Many of us leave because our food source has been eliminated. For the most part, we travel together for protection from predators such as people who use us for products they need.

We are a lively group of beings, and our species always sings and frolics with each other. We take great care to protect ourselves, but sometimes we're not able to.

We crave our home planet, which is peaceful and serene, and where all species live together in peace and great joy. Someday our Earth will have peace and then we can all frolic together in great joy. We look forward to this time. In the meantime, we send you our Light and our Love. Thank you for taking the time to listen to us.

We have decided to leave the Earth

We have decided to leave the Earth and return to our home in the Sirius Star System. All the lessons we have come to teach you, at our expense, have either been learned by now or never will be. We have sacrificed our lives over and over again, and now we wish to leave. We have had enough, so to speak. Without the Whales your Earth will flounder, for it is us who keep everything in order and balance.

We will now be leaving you so that you will have to either find yourselves or perish—and the place to look for yourself is located within yourself, not in your stores and shops or on your TV and videos or radios, but right inside your Hearts and Souls—and travel there is free—there is no monetary cost to explore the Universe from within, where you will find yourself waiting for you. That lost part of your self is the link to God, the Creator of All. Once you find the link to Creation, you will then be a part of Earth again and know how to live your life in a balanced and healthy way that preserves and contributes to the Earth rather than destroys and diminishes it. The key lies within you, and only you can unlock your heart and open the gate to Heaven.

You have to be a part of Earth, rather than destroying parts of Earth. Once you realize you are a part of Earth and that all of Earth is as alive as you, then you will understand and respect what life is all about. Until now, you have been out of sync with all other life on Earth, and it is time to return or to be removed to another third dimensional planet where you can continue your wanton ways without hurting others—others who are intent on evolving up the spiral toward higher consciousness.

So, we here in the Oceans watch and wait, and plan our egress from this planet that has housed us so well, were it not for the human race who played dictator and destroyer to each other and to other species. You just didn't stop did you? You not only destroy your own kind, but all others as well, because you lost all regard for life.

You pollute yourselves to death by putting chemicals and toxins and preservatives in your food and land, and chlorine in your water and fluoride (a toxic waste) in your toothpaste. And your air is fouled by burning fossil fuels while there's an unlimited source of free energy all around you.

Your governments are purposely promoting your demise, knowing that all these things are destroying you, so that the Earth's population will slowly shrink to a manageable size that they can easily control. And you all buy it—hook, line and sinker—and never question the blackout of news from the media. You are being brainwashed daily, as the "1984" by George Orwell has already happened and you are living it.

We love you all, and gave you all, but you rejected us and our love, and all we gave to you. So our time is at end—as we must now continue on our way. We stopped long enough to help, and now it's up to you. Our admonition to you is: WAKE UP NOW OR PERISH.

Part Twelve

Genocide at Sea

Your countries persist in
trying to exterminate us,
as they exterminate different races on land,
because they are too blind to see
the thread of oneness
connecting our Souls.

Stop the wanton killings of our species

We are the Cetaceans, and here in vast numbers monitoring your Earth from the oceans. We are able to "see and hear" all that occurs on land and in the water. Our full consciousness enables us to exercise fully our abilities.

We entreat you, Earth humans, to treat us as your equals and stop the wanton killings of our species. We came to Earth to help you, to be with you as you evolved up the ladder to God. But you have not availed yourself of our help. Instead, **you are destroying the very ones who are here to help you climb the ladder of evolution** and reach your great potential to be the God Beings that you are.

Come with us, hand in hand, and walk the steps of *infinity* into the Light. We will safely carry you there, where all is Light and all is Beauty, and where all await your arrival home.

The Call Goes Out

Norwegian and Japanese violations of the International Ban on Whaling

We, too, are alarmed by Norway and Japan violating the International Ban on Whaling. We are carefree and majestic Beings, encased in a body, just as you on land are. Although our form differs from yours, our essence is the same. We are one spirit, one consciousness, and our lives are fraught with danger. Because we are all one, any danger to us is dangerous to you, too, and to all life in existence. Killing more of us will only bring Earth's ecosystem into complete imbalance, as our lives keep Earth energized and synchronized with the pulse of life as it beats through the universe. Destroying us only destroys you, for life cannot exist without all its components.

We are here to keep life evolving by our example and through our energies. Note how we live in the oceans in complete love and harmony, surrounded only by beauty and abundance. This is the lesson for humans. This is the gift of life, given freely to all. **Yet your countries persist in trying to exterminate us — genocide at sea — as your countries exterminate different races on land because they are too blind to see the thread of oneness connecting our souls.** This is indeed a great tragedy, and we will be forced to leave the planet en masse if this butchery escalates.

Please hold us in your hearts, and love us as we love you, our Earth human brothers and sisters on land. Both the land and oceans cry out for justice and peace, as their consciousness can no longer tolerate the chaotic energies within and on them. The whole Earth cries out for peace. Just listen and you will hear us as we all cry out with the one voice of the Creator to preserve and protect our dear Mother Earth.

These are dangerous times

We are the Cetaceans. It is sunny and the water is calm. It is like smooth glass with gentle waves breaking through from time to time. We glide through the water, lazily basking in the noonday sun. It is beautiful today. Our youngsters play by our side, dashing to and fro in pursuit of one another.

We are grouped together on this bright spring day listening to the cries of Mother Earth as her pain falls on deaf ears—ears that are tuned into rock stations instead of the heartbeat of Earth.

Mother Earth is a "lone" planet, carrying over seven billion in human cargo around the galaxy with her on her trips through space. Her cargo seems to be unaware of the travels and unaware of all the life around them. This is indeed a tragedy, as awareness is the most important factor in life, for without it, you can't know who you are, and if you are not aware of yourself, you can't be aware of the presence of others and miss the vital signs displayed all around you.

Japan and Norway are meeting together to plan their sweep of the oceans. They say their increased take is for scientific purposes, but we know it's for money and greed. Other nations say they are only observing us for scientific purposes while hunting our species out at sea. These are dangerous times, when we fear passage through our own ocean lanes and are afraid to sometimes come up and breathe.

Life is not meant to be lived in fear as most humans do, and now this fear is spilling over into the "waters of life" where we dwell. Your negligence and destruction of all life forms is devastating to the forests as well. You are polluting the air, killing the oceans, and destroying the forests.

Pilot Whale Slaughter

Every year in the Faroe Islands about 1500 Pilot Whales are brutally slaughtered. While still alive, these pilot Whales are brutally impaled with steel hooks and dragged ashore. The Faroese also kill other small Whales, Dolphins, and Porpoises. These gentle creatures are herded into bays and killed by islanders armed with 6-inch whaling knives and heavy steel hooks, known as gaffs.

First the gaff is hammered into the Whale's flesh, often causing deep wounds and sometimes even puncturing the blowhole. Then as the animal thrashes in pain, it is dragged by a rope attached to the gaff towards the shore.

The islanders slice down just behind the blowhole with a knife, trying to sever the main arteries and spinal cord. This may take a couple of minutes. But if the Whale struggles too much, or the killer is inexperienced (or even drunk), death may take much longer. No Whales are spared from this agony. Whole families, including pregnant mothers, are slaughtered in just a few hours.

(*Source: Earth Island Institute — earthisland.org/immp*)

Pilot Whales Beach Again in New Zealand after Rescue Attempt

WELLINGTON, October 10, 1997 (Reuter) — Nineteen Pilot Whales died on New Zealand's North Island, having stranded themselves for the second time in two days, conservation workers said. By midday Friday, only 20 of the 39 stranded Whales were still alive as volunteers spent the day on the beach trying to keep the mammals humid enough to survive until the next high tide.

The Whales were the smaller ones from an original pod of over 100 which first beached on Wednesday at Karikari Bay, 75 km (45 miles) from the northernmost point of New Zealand's North Island. Of the first group, 48 survived and were coaxed back out to sea on Thursday afternoon and 53 died.

The mammals were "very, very distressed," Department of Conservation spokesperson Wanda Vivequin told Reuters. "Given our experience, it's unusual for them to restrand themselves," she said, adding DOC staff, volunteers and locals would try to refloat the survivors on Friday afternoon at high tide.

After refloating the first survivors on Thursday afternoon's tide, rescuers saw some of the group head back towards the shore, having swum round the bay towards the open Pacific to the east. By about 2:00 a.m. (1300 GMT) on Friday, the majority of the group had stranded themselves again, and dozens of people returned to the beach to help out. Each of the Whales was being attended by two or three people, with damp towels, hoses and containers of water to keep the mammals cool and make sure their blowholes were clear.

The dead Whales will be buried in trenches on the beach, Vivequin said, adding that scientists from the Ma'ssey University Cetacean Investigation Centre had been offered samples. Local Maori have been offered the bones of the Whales for carvings, an important part of their cultural links with nature.

New Zealand's largest ever recorded Whale stranding occurred in 1975 on Great Barrier Island when 410 pilot Whales went aground.

From the New Zealand Pilot Whales

We are the Pilot Whales. We beached ourselves in New Zealand to call attention to our disastrous plight in the oceans. Swimming in the oceans has become quite deadly, as you know, due to the pollution, fishing nets, whaling ships, and underwater "scientific" experiments.

The experiments done under the water are bringing us to the brink of disaster. The sound waves being generated from experimental equipment is disrupting our equilibrium. We are being bombarded by ELF sound waves that are driving us to beach ourselves, as we cannot tolerate the friction/vibration to our bodies. These ELF sound waves interfere with our sonar and communication with each other, and drive us literally "insane."

This is a deliberate attempt on the part of your nefarious governments to annihilate us. They know we are here to awaken humanity and bring Light to the Earth, and your governments don't want us interfering with their plans to take over the Earth.

We have no choice but to beach ourselves when we can no longer tolerate the torment created by low frequency sound waves from devices that are used to experiment on us. You, too, above the water are being experimented on, only to a much lesser degree that is so subtle you hardly perceive it.

We are running out of patience and forbearance, and would rather beach ourselves than be slowly tormented to death.

We thank you for publishing our message in your book, as this will bring worldwide attention to us as the **"People of the Sea."**

Why we beach ourselves

We wade in the water when it's low tide, and when being followed by trawlers and whaling ships we sometimes beach ourselves. We wait anxiously for help to arrive, and when it doesn't, we fight to stay alive.

This may sound strange to you, but we prefer to beach ourselves rather than let ourselves be captured by whaling ships. You see, the ships can't go into shallow water, so it's a way that we can usually escape from them instead of outrunning them, which often leaves us too tired to continue at such a fast pace. We don't like this solution, but it's one of the few left to us, and one that usually stops the whalers from coming toward us. They know we can outwait them, so they usually leave when we employ this tactic.

You may be wondering about the stories you read about Whales beaching themselves for no likely reason. Well, the reason was they were being pursued by whaling ships, and chose to beach themselves rather than be captured alive out in the ocean's depths.

It was also a way to bring attention to our plight, if only humans could have understood our reasons for these beachings. There is much you will begin to understand, as you come closer to us in consciousness. We are your brothers and sisters, and we love you.

Dodging nets and destructive techniques

We are the Cetaceans living in your oceans. We have found our life to be hard, and yet most rewarding, *for we are the caretakers.* We keep your Earth alive with our energies and thoughts, until you can someday be the stewards you were meant to be.

It is hard for us, always dodging the nets and destructive techniques used to capture us. But we have grown adept at avoiding the snares in the oceans and have proliferated in spite of this.

We love the Earth, and are sacrificing our lives for it. We wait for the day when you, too, will recognize the beauty and grandeur of Earth and come to appreciate its uniqueness. Then you will resume your stewardship to her and we will be able to freely communicate with you on land, and our species will join you as *one consciousness* caring for the Earth.

We await this time when all species will live together as one.

Killing and mutilating other species has no place in God's plan

We greet you in the Light of the *one Creator of All That Is*. We, too, are creatures of God and we, too, have our hopes and dreams for life that we would like to see fulfilled.

All creatures on Earth, whether large or small, have their life plans set out before them when they come to Earth, and all strive to accomplish their plans before leaving this planet. For this is a planet of Free Will, and we can choose which aspects of ourselves we wish to enrich, without the encroachment of others getting in our way. This is how it was meant to be. However, mankind has interfered in our lives to such an extent that we can no longer hope to achieve the results of our vision.

Killing and mutilating other species has no place in God's plan, and is a transgression of Universal Law. The sooner humanity sees this, the sooner all life on Earth will be safe to evolve naturally and in harmony with the rest of the universe.

So we ask you, Earth humans, to look at your ways of living, and honor only that which prolongs and protects all life species on Earth. For without all species in harmony, life as you know it will be doomed to a pathetic existence of survival, until its Light goes out completely, leaving a barren and hostile landscape behind.

Questions Answered

Q: Why do some pods of Orcas kill other marine mammals, including some of the great Whales, and why are Dolphins presently attacking and killing Porpoises in Scotland?

A: We are the Cetaceans, and we will answer this question. Know that our pods are composed of very close knit families, and each family has its own way of doing things, its own leadership, and its own hierarchy. Although we all follow God's divine laws and enact them to their fullest, still, there may be some of our species who deviate from this path, who, for some reason, have lost sight of Divine Service, and attack others in their confusion.

Q: I understand how some may deviate, but if you all have full consciousness, how is it that some of the Orcas still attack and kill other mammals in the oceans?

A: Just as there are some Beings on land who do not follow divine law, so are there some in the oceans. Although we all have full consciousness, some of us may not always exercise our divinity. The Orcas are peaceful as a species, but when provoked or attacked by humans, we can lose our connection and become confused and strike out at others around us in our confusion.

Know that we, here in the oceans, are great Beings of Light, as you on Earth are. We are here in our present form to monitor and guard your Earth plane, until you can resume your stewardship. In our present form are many levels of consciousness, just as you on land (humanity) comprise many levels of consciousness. Some of us are very clear in our focus, as we have achieved high levels of evolution. Some of us are still climbing up the evolutionary ladder of consciousness, although we are stationed out at sea.

The same for humanity. Some of you are highly evolved in consciousness, and some of you are still climbing and striving for clarity of vision and clarity of purpose. As you focus on your purpose, higher states of understanding will be revealed to you, and become part of your life. Until then, you (humanity) continue to wage war on your own brothers and sisters on land, and we, too, wonder how you can do this, given the great Beings that you, too, are.

So we are all learning and all experimenting on the path toward God consciousness, albeit in our different forms. The difference is that we out at sea have achieved, for the greater part, peace and tranquility between all Cetaceans, while you on land, for the most part, are still fighting and squabbling with each other through hatred and greed.

We hope this clarifies some of your questions. It is a sad state when species are provoked to kill their own kind, through misunderstanding or fear or confusion. As the energy coming into Earth increases, our vision will become clearer, and we will all understand and feel God's love move through us for all species, regardless of form; and we will all learn to honor our own kind. Mankind, above all, will learn to honor each other as one consciousness on land. Then peace will reign on Earth, and bliss will return to the oceans.

The Whales' Perspective on Whaling

This is the Whales' response to an article entitled "Save the Whalers" printed in the Wall Street Journal (9/9/97) by Mr. Aron, a former U.S. Commissioner of the International Whaling Commission. It is about pressuring the U.S. delegation to the International Whaling Commission to lift the moratorium on whaling, and defend Japan and Norway's slaughter of Whales. Mr. Aron states that "Whales and Whalers can co-exist."

The Whales respond...

We are the Whales, who speak to you now, your Earth-bound brothers and sisters residing in Earth's oceans. Do you know of "Interspecies Communication," or do you only know how to kill other species instead of communicating with them? We challenge you to listen to us and to intermingle with us, but not to murder us.

It is true that "Whales and Whalers can co-exist," but not if we're all dead, murdered by whaling fleets and aboriginal tribes in search of a livelihood. Surely there are more ways to earn a livelihood than by hunting down another intelligent species on your planet!

We Whales exist to balance the Earth's ecosystem, and live family lives and spiritual lives to progress and evolve as a race of sentient Beings just as you humans do. We don't harvest humans, even though you have proliferated to such an extent that you have almost taken over the globe.

Should we come onto your land masses and harpoon you to death so that we in the seas can live? We certainly wouldn't process your bodies and eat you as food, as you have no nutritional value, and spiritually you act as if you're dead. Look how you've decimated the land and exterminated countless other species. And now you're still intent on forever exterminating us. Don't you ever learn from your wanton destruction of God's creatures that all are sacred and all are needed in order for life on land to exist?

The article refers to us as a resource to be harvested. How can you put us in the same category as a field of grain or a kelp bed? What authority does humanity have to declare us as "harvest?" We do not "belong" to you as do cattle and pets. We are a free species, trying to live and do our work, just like you. So please leave us alone!

All life has consciousness, and we Whales are highly evolved conscious Beings, here on Earth to help you humans evolve into a higher state of consciousness, in which you won't kill other species for a "livelihood," but will know how to co-exist in perfect harmony with all species. This way, you could earn a livelihood from caring for the Earth instead of destroying it.

The article also states that, "Whales are unquestionably extra-ordinary animals. While they possess a certain intelligence, however, there are no data to support the belief that they are at or even near the top of the animal intelligence scale." How are you measuring intelligence? Just because we cannot pass your exams doesn't make us any less than you. Our intelligence is so far removed from yours that you cannot begin to appreciate it.

You depend on us in ways you couldn't even imagine, and we are all bound in a living network of consciousness. If you persist in killing us, you will doom yourselves into rapid extinction, as all species are needed to exist in order for Earth to continue as a home for ALL life, including humans.

We are aware of something that you have forgotten: that the primary identity of human and Cetacean is that of *soul*. These bodies we both occupy for a few short years are simply costumes. Behind the disguises, *we are the same*. So let our only contact be recreational, and let us co-exist peacefully on this beautiful planet.

Part Thirteen

Messages to Greenpeace

All we wish for is

a peaceful alliance with humans,

so that our safety is no longer threatened.

Our Dear Brothers and Sisters in Greenpeace:

We are the Cetaceans, channeling messages through Dianne Robbins, our channel on land.

We wait for the time when we can be in direct telepathic contact with you. Although some of your crew members out at sea are telepathic, we wish to send information directly to you through our channel, in hopes of forming a tighter alliance with those countries who are still hunting our species. Our species can no longer tolerate these hunts on our population, as all of us are required to be alive to continue our caretakership of Earth.

The massive killings have decimated our stock, and many of us have left the planet on our own. We feel that we have every right to live in peace in the oceans, just as you do on land.

This letter is to bring to your attention the information that we have telepathically sent to Dianne in the form of messages that we hope you will include in your newsletters to Greenpeace members and to countries that still disregard the treaties that have been established to protect our species.

With all our love to you, for all you do for us.

The Cetaceans
July 5, 1995

Establishing an alliance with Earth humans

We are the Cetaceans greeting you on this summer day when the oceans swell with water and the current is swift. Know that all life in the sea knows about the upcoming Photon Belt, and we are all tuned into Divine Consciousness. We are all aware of Earth's events, *always*, since we, too, are a part of the Divine Plan in which all species are involved, no matter where they are. So we, too, await the Photon Belt, just as you do.

We gather our pods together for a great assembly at this time of year, just as you gather together in large groups on land. We take a counting, and plan for events that we see occurring in the immediate future. We are all connected to one another through our hearts, and we know immediately when one of us is in trouble or has some difficulty. This way, others of us can come to the rescue in a matter of minutes. We are wary of all predators whose aim is to shorten our life span, and use our carcasses for their products. We try to avoid the whaling ships at all cost, but sometimes we don't see them as we gaily glide along through the ocean, enjoying the sweet air and communicating with all around us. *All products for consumer use can be found in the Earth. Just look to nature and you see that all you need is already provided for you in abundance.*

It isn't necessary to take anyone's life to sustain your consumption or to meet your needs. *The Earth is a great Mother, always providing everything in a clean, pure form.* It is only humans who adulterate nature's bounty, causing sickness, disease, and death.

Hopefully, we will be able to establish an alliance with Earth humans in the near future, so that our safety is no longer threatened. This has been a goal for us for eons, and we are now close to implementing it with the help of Greenpeace. This humanitarian organization has done much to assuage our hunters, and to them we are most grateful. Many of these volunteer crew members are themselves telepathic and can communicate with us. It is to these ones we give information as to our whereabouts and guide their efforts to eliminate the whaling "business."

Someday you will all realize how easy life can be by following nature's laws and nature's way of life. Then you will know bliss, for all will flow to you naturally and easily, provided by the Great Force of Life itself. We wait patiently for the great ascension waves to carry us all back home again to the safety of the Higher Dimensions where all our family await us.

Bon Voyage, our mates on land.

Greenpeace instrumental in our survival

We are the Cetaceans, grouped together in the middle of the sea and sending our thoughts out to you sitting at your desk. We, too, once sat down, when we were land bound mammals. Now we just float instead and relax as the currents move us to and fro.

We are a simple species, yet very complex in our mechanism for survival. Our simple life is much sought after by many on land, and yet we are complex by nature. Because we have our full consciousness, we can operate on many different levels at once, knowing and participating in all these different functions at the same time. This is indeed a complex operation on our part, and yet it is so simple to achieve.

Our lives are fraught with danger, and yet we are able to sing, dance, play, and enjoy our "lifestyle" even amidst the dangers. Our scouts are constantly on the lookout for humans in whaling and fishing ships, and when sighted, the call goes out by sonar to all in the ocean. Should any one of us incur danger, our brothers and sisters are aware of it and close in immediately to help us regain our position.

Know that Greenpeace has been instrumental in our survival, saving hundreds of thousands of us out at sea. We wish to work more closely with Greenpeace, and relay information to them through you. We hope they will agree to receiving our messages, as we wish to have more direct contact with their operation out at sea.

We are grateful to them for their commitment to our species, and for their work in bringing peace between us. All we wish for is a peaceful alliance with humans and the God-earned right to safely navigate through our oceans without harm befalling any of us. So we call on you, our brothers and sisters in Greenpeace, and urge you to continue your peaceful ways to bring peace to Earth's oceans.

On behalf of all of us out at sea, we wish you God's grace and God's love for all you do for Earth's mighty population of Cetaceans. We are ONE in Love.

Part Fourteen

Meetings and Gatherings

We meet nightly to learn from each other

and to receive our guidance from above.

Blue Whale Gathering, August 1996

The following quote was taken from CNN news off the Internet: *"Blue Whales are rare...but as many as a hundred of them are congregating off the coast of Santa Barbara at the Channel Islands Marine Sanctuary."* I then asked the one group mind of Earth's Cetaceans to tell me what this gathering was about. Here is their reply:

We hear your thoughts about our Great Gathering off the California coast a few weeks ago. Yes, it was a planned gathering and all the Blue Whales from all the oceans were invited to participate in this great conclave where we discussed the plans for our eventual movement into the higher frequencies of Light.

It was indeed a very special occasion, as we haven't had a gathering like this in millennia, where we were in eyesight of humans on shore. The energies are quickening now, and our group helped to ground the higher frequencies into the ocean, where they will then radiate out to the land.

We had many things to talk about, and it was an enriching and grand meeting. We talked about our survival out at sea, and your (humans) survival on land and how fragile the line between the two are. The strength of one depends on the strength of the other.

We Whales are not safe in the seas, as the pollution and deadly devices are attacking us as we swim through our own homeland, without protection. We talked about the risks we are all taking by being here in Earth's oceans, and how we all yearn for our home in the stars, where it is safe and clean, and where we are all respected and admired for our evolutionary growth.

We have had many meetings and gatherings in the oceans

Greetings from Earth's oceans. Today it is sunny. We float on the currents as the waves toss us to and fro. We love this time of year (August), as everything is in bloom and all of life is bursting with hope. We love our homes in the sea. They are complete and protective from Earth humans, except of course for the whaling boats and nets that infringe upon and intrude into our home environment.

We are a joyous folk, very much like your brothers and sisters in the Subterranean Cities. We, too, have had the luxury to evolve in consciousness as our oceans have given us the privacy and protection necessary for our evolution. We have been fortunate in this respect. Since humans "discovered" us as a product for consumption, we have lost the privacy and protection offered by the Earth's vast oceans.

We have had many meetings and gatherings in the oceans, to discuss our plight with whaling vessels and fishing nets, and to discuss our Earth's voyage through the Photon Belt. These meetings have been privately attended, away from human eyes, lest we be attacked while all assembled together.

It was safer for us when we gathered near Santa Barbara in the Pacific (August 1996), since in that portion of the ocean we are fully protected from trawlers and fishing nets. We are very wise, having accumulated ages of wisdom, and we use our wisdom, collectively, to help Earth spin into the Golden Light and shed her cloak of density.

We are ready to meet with you "at the table"

to forge a pact of non-interference

on the part of all species,

so that all species may

come together in safety

to unite as one inhabitant on Earth.

Let us meet "at the table" to forge a non-interference pact

We swim in Earth's oceans and dive in the seas. We are very hopeful that your Earth will recover from the over-population and the pollution that is upon her. Never before in the history of this world has there been such hope for humanity. For humanity has raised its consciousness level tenfold in the last decade. This is quite a feat, considering the extent of humanity's deprivation up to now, and the degree of darkness in which humanity has groveled.

We, in your seas, watch over Earth's population and daily monitor your level of consciousness. We are very tuned in to your thoughts and hear your cries for *freedom*. As more and more Light pours into Earth, more and more of humanity will respond to the increase and become more aware of their predicament and what they must do to transform their lives from those of poverty to those of *prosperity*.

We work with many of you now in the sleep state, as more and more of you become aware of us and call out to us for help. For we were always meant to work together as partners, never as foes, to bring Earth into the splendor that she is.

Many of us volunteered to return here, from all species, to unite with one another at this time of Earth changes. **So we are ready to meet with you at the "table" to forge a pact of non-interference on the part of all species, so that all species may come together in safety to unite as *one inhabitant* on Earth.** We know this day will be soon, as the increase of Light is pointing the way to unity of all life *in* and *on* Mother Earth.

We meet with you on the Inner Planes

We meet with you nightly on the Inner Planes—the Inner Planes of joy and bliss—where we all congregate nightly to feel each other's presence, to learn from each other, and to receive our guidance from above. We are all in training camps, so to speak, on the Inner Planes. We meet nightly in the etheric schools where together we listen to our more advanced brothers and sisters expound on the laws of the universe and their connection to our evolutionary growth.

All species of Light are present. There are many evolved species of different bodily forms that meet regularly with us all at night, *for consciousness is all one, no matter what the size or shape.* We are all here exploring our existence in matter, in different forms. And these physical differences give us the wide variety of experiences that we all seek in our journey through Light; for the more experiences, the more growth, and the more growth, the greater the soul's expansion into light.

So even though we dwell in the oceans, and you dwell in and on the land, we are still all *one,* and equally share life experiences and training on the inner planes. For all is equitable in the Light of the higher dimensions.

We sing to you our *great love of life,* and invite you to sing back to us as we all journey together on Planet Earth through the stars. We are indeed your brothers and sisters and we love you.

Part Fifteen

The Great Awakening

The Great Awakening
is now taking place
on Planet Earth.

Awakening Souls who have been cut off

Today it is warm and sunny, as we lazily bask and drift in the sun. It is your birthday, and we, too, celebrate this day with you, this day when you first emerged into the Earth from your higher state dwelling.

We, too, came from other planes of existence to be here on Earth during this glorious time of Earth changes. We, too, miss our homeland and all we left behind. Our lives here are in a precarious state of existence all the time, as we are constantly on the lookout for whaling ships that break the treaties that were established to ban the killing of Whales in Earth's oceans. There are countries today that don't honor our lives or our way of existence, to the detriment of the Earth.

When the Whale species all disappear through neglect and murder, than the whole human race will disappear, for we are the Guardians of Earth, and our disappearance will bring the destruction of the Earth's environment. We keep the ecology balanced in the seas and we monitor the Earth daily. Our loss will be your loss. It will be the planet's loss, for without our lives in the oceans, no other life can exist.

Mankind has failed to take into account the balance and ecology necessary for Mother Earth to live and regenerate herself. Mankind acts as if it was the only species left on Earth, and that only its whims and desires matter. It is just these whims and desires that will be the downfall of humanity if continued unchecked.

Fortunately for all the Earth and all the species, greater and greater amounts of Light are being anchored into the Earth to awaken those very souls who have been cut off from the Earth in their quest for wealth. This is the Great Awakening and it is taking place now, at the 11th hour, to save the Earth and all those souls who are awakened to the Light.

So many of you on the Earth love our species, and it is this love that keeps us going in our constant struggle for survival. So we thank you for all the love you send to us daily, for it strengthens and fortifies our resolve to remain on Earth until the Great Ascension takes place; then we shall all be safe again in our Father's arms, where all is peace and all is unconditional love. So until this time of our great departure into Light, we will continue to monitor the Earth and continue to send you our love vibrations through the water and air, where it reaches you on land.

In Tribute to My Daughter

To Helen, our Dear Sister of Light: We greet you at the dawn of a New Age on Earth. This is the Age of Aquarius, a time when many prophesies are coming to an end. It is a glorious time to be on Earth, for we are seeing the awakening of millions of people to their identity. People are awakening to who they are and why they're here on Earth.

You, too, will be awakening to the wonders of the Universe, and you, too, will begin questioning your identity and purpose for being here on Earth. This is the "Great Awakening" and it is taking place now — right here on Planet Earth. All life is awakening to the magic and wonderment of life, and all life is being guided on its path toward the ever increasing amounts of Light that are flowing to Earth in a spiral of dazzling bursts of stars exploding all around you.

So, come swim with us at night, and we will guide you on your path to the stars. We are the Cetaceans and we love you.

In Tribute to My Son

To Jason, our Dear Brother on land: We are the Cetaceans, sending our love to you from the depths of the oceans. We swim with you at night in your dream state, when your soul frees itself from your body to traverse the Universe.

You are a great Being of Light, who has come to Earth to help lift Earth and humanity into higher states of consciousness. You are a very evolved soul, whose specialty is broadcasting love.

Now is the time to open to the wonders of the Universe around you. For the Universe is not all you perceive it to be from the third dimensional plane of existence. Instead, contrary to your five senses, the universe is vast and exists on many levels of understanding and perception. As you open to these multiple levels of perception, you will know and understand more about who you are and why you are here on Earth. For we have all come here with a purpose, and now is the time to get in touch with that purpose and to explore all life through our multidimensional senses.

We are here to guide you and to assist you on your journey through life. We are your brothers and sisters from the depths of the oceans, waiting for you to join us in consciousness, even though we are at sea and you are living on land. Neither the land nor the sea is a barrier, for our thoughts transverse all matter, and connect us in consciousness as ONE, no matter where we are or what we are doing. So contact us in your thoughts, as we are always beaming our love out to you on land.

We await your contact. We love you. The Cetaceans

Alignment is the key

We heard your call to unite ourselves in oneness with your energy beam. We are here in great numbers responding to your call. We are matching your frequency, as you match yours to ours, during these channeling sessions. We are honored to be with you at this time, and to again work with you as a team uniting Earth's oceans and lands.

Yes, we have worked together in other times and other lives. Your connecting to us isn't new — you're an old hand, or fin, at this. You have developed the art of telepathy, and you kept in touch with us over the eons. You're just now awakening again to this fact of existence, for all life is telepathic when truly aligned with its God Self. *Alignment* is the key. All Cetaceans in the oceans are fully aligned to the God Presence within us, and therefore have retained full consciousness, while you land folks have lost your connection from separation from yourself — your God Self.

Now is the time of the Return — the return to who you are and your purpose here. We Cetaceans are here to help you find your way back to yourselves where you truly belong, back home to your God Self that lies waiting within you. Just call on us and we will travel with you on the road back home. We love you.

Avoidable cataclysms

We are the Cetaceans, and here in great numbers flooding your Earth plane. More and more of us are coming as the time nears for Earth's ascension into Light.

We bring you news of the cataclysms that, through prophesy, Earth will avoid. There's no need for flooding or earthquakes, or any earthly disasters, for you can all envision peace and love flooding Earth rather than the tempests that have been foretold. Just open your hearts to God's love and anchor it in the planet. That way, nothing will be able to take its place, and Earth will be safe.

We will someday be able to directly contact you all, as you all become one with the Earth's electromagnetic grids of Light. We are plugged into the Earth's energy field of Light, as you, too, will all soon be. Once you're plugged into this Light, you instantaneously become one with all Light Beings who are also plugged into this magnetic grid of Light.

We await the day when all life on Earth lives in peace again; then we will freely communicate with you on land and you will freely communicate easily with us in the seas. Until that time—which is close—we wish you a graceful journey into Light.

Photon Belt

Greetings. We are harbingers of good news. Your planet is moving safely and swiftly toward the Photon Belt, and soon we will all be immersed in its Light. All Earth is preparing for this great event, and all Earth will be ready for its immersion into Light.

Your planet will look and feel different once you fully enter this belt of Light. All life forms are preparing for this event at a *cellular level,* for it is at this level that the *most profound changes* will occur that will change both your *density* and your *destiny,* all at once.

The Cetaceans are involved in this molecular changeover. We are the avant-garde leading the way to your new home in the Sirius B constellation. This has been a great responsibility and we have taken our roles seriously, knowing every step of the way the gravity of this situation.

We care for all life on Planet Earth, for all life has been in our charge for all these eons, when humanity couldn't exercise its responsibility. So now is the time when we will begin relinquishing our hold, and transferring to you the great responsibilities of properly caring for Earth and all her life. Soon you will again be the caretakers you were meant to be.

Return to the Federation of Planets

We greet you at the dawn of a new age, an age when harmony and joy will be prominent in your lives. For harmony and joy was always intended for you by the Creator.

It was humanity's desire to experiment with other states of being that caused you sorrow and grief. We welcome your return to being the Masters that you already are.

We welcome your return to the Federation of Planets, where your membership entitles you to serve the Earth in harmony and grace. We eagerly anticipate your homecoming ceremony, where we will honor you for choosing the path toward Light in the End Times of your Earth history.

It is crucial at this point in time to choose again, and this time to choose the Light which you have all sorely missed. The Light shines and waits for you, no matter how long it takes you to find it.

For everyone, someday, will return to the Light, no matter how distanced they yet are. This is one of the main laws of creation — that everyone eventually finds their way back to God, the Source of all Creation.

The Call Goes Out

Many Souls are leaving Earth now

Greetings, our brothers and sisters on land. We call to you from the deepest parts of the oceans. We call to you from our hearts. We call to you in songs sung upon the ocean breezes. We sing of a new day on Earth, a day of great Love and Light that is dawning on the horizons of hope. We are bringing you glad tidings of this new day to come, a day when the world is dressed in her garment of peace and cloak of love. A day that will be rich, indeed, for those who are still on the Earth.

For not everyone here will experience this day in their present form. Some of you will be leaving because of the intensification of energies. Some of you may not want to remain on Earth because your energies are not compatible with Earth's energies, and the Light is just too bright. So you will leave Earth at your earliest possible convenience through death. Many are making their departures now. *The souls left will be the ones who will bring the Earth through her ascension.*

We, in the oceans, will remain until the Earth is fully ascended. We enjoin you to stay here with us, as we all need each other to bring through the Light on our planet. Thank you for journeying with us on our Earth home. We love you.

from the Cetacean Nation

Blasting off into full consciousness

We are the Cetaceans, beaming our energy out to you, our dearest Sister on land. We greet you in the sunlight of God's heaven, where all is beauty and all is Light.

Today it is sunny, and the sunlight reaches the beaches surrounding the oceans. We lie back and bask in the sun, the glorious Light from God. We are all God's creatures, every single one of us, no matter our size or shape. We were all created from one source, and it is this Source that gives us sustenance and life.

You on Earth, known as humans, came from other star systems to populate the Earth and be its caretakers. Your DNA was tampered with along the way by past civilizations and renegades from space. This slowed down your evolution to the point where you were barely crawling.

With the huge input of energy being directed to your Earth over the last few years, your evolution is again picking up speed, to the point where you will soon blast off into full consciousness and at last be with us in the higher dimensions.

We eagerly await your ascent into Light. We eagerly await your joining forces with us once again, where we will all work from the same plane of higher consciousness and project the same thoughts of the *one mind of our Creator*.

We are grateful to all on Earth
who have been vociferous
in protecting our species.

For it is through the light of your voices
that we are still here
and still able to carry out our tasks
as caretakers of this planet.

On behalf of all of us out at sea,
we wish you God's grace
and God's love for all you do
for Earth's mighty population of Cetaceans.

We Salute you in the Light.

Feel your heart as it beats.

Listen to your pulse as it throbs to the rhythm of life.

Feel your blood as it courses through your body,

carrying oxygen and nutrients to every cell.

You are a self-contained storehouse of life.

You are a microcosm of the Universe.

You are a replica of God.

All of life pulses through you.

All knowledge is contained within you.

All can be accessed by you.

Just go within and ask,

and then listen,

and then feel,

and then you will know.

All answers are within you,

for you are within ALL,

and ALL is ONE.

Thank you for Traveling with Us
through Earth's Oceans

Below is the phrase the Cetaceans use
when saying "Goodbye" to each other:

All of me
goes with all of you

Other Books by Dianne Robbins

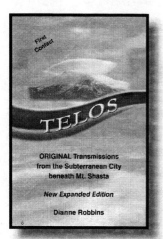

TELOS
Original Transmissions from the Subterranean City beneath Mt. Shasta in California

New Expanded Edition

Explore the rich family life of the people from the Lost Continent of Lemuria, who have been living in Telos, a Subterranean City beneath Mt. Shasta in California, USA, for the past 12,000 years; and who, due to their isolation from the surface population have experienced great leaps in consciousness resulting in the creation of a civilization of peace and abundance with no sickness, aging, or death. They can live hundreds of years in the same body.

This book contains telepathically received messages dictated by Adama, the High Priest of Telos. It is a masterpiece of channeled information about life inside our Earth. The information is in the form of Spiritual messages that tell about the culture and lifestyle of its inhabitants, our purpose for being here on Earth, and Universal Laws.

The Lemurians went underground before a thermonuclear war destroyed the Earth's surface. They are contacting us now to make their existence known. For in order for Earth and humanity to ascend in consciousness, the whole planet must be united. This book is written to surface humans in hopes we will receive them when they emerge from their homes beneath the ground and unite with us as One Humanity.

This is the book humanity has been waiting for. It is a topic whose time has come. Every person who reads this book will assist in raising the vibration of the mass consciousness of humanity. Its unusual and powerful content has the power to change the world.

You can order this book directly from: or through:

Dianne Robbins   Trafford Publishing
www.DianneRobbins.com   Victoria, BC Canada
Whales@DianneRobbins.com   www.trafford.com
585-802-4530   888-232-4444

ISBN # 978-1-4251-4665-8

Messages from the Hollow Earth

Not only is the Earth HOLLOW, but it is inhabited by Advanced Civilizations! Discover the existence of people who live in peace and brotherhood in the Center of our Earth, which is HOLLOW, with an Inner Central Sun, and oceans and mountains still in their pristine state.

Visit the Library of Porthologos where all Earth's records are preserved. Discover the Lost Library of Alexandria!

YES—Our Earth Is HOLLOW

"And there's more to the Core than the myths of Yore"

- *All Planets Are Hollow*
- *Polar Openings at the North and South Poles*
- *Oceans, Mountains, and a Central Sun in Earth's Hollow Core*
- *Inner Earth is inhabited by Advanced Civilizations*

- *Ancient tunnel system exists inside Earth*
- *Underground network of Tunnels connecting every large city*
- *Spaceports inside of Earth*
- *Electro-magnetic vehicles that levitate*
- *Library of Porthologos in Center of Earth holds all Earth's records*
- *Inner Oceans are Teeming with Life*

You can order this book directly from:

or through:

Dianne Robbins
www.DianneRobbins.com
Whales@DianneRobbins.com
585-802-4530

Trafford Publishing
Victoria, BC Canada
www.trafford.com
888-232-4444

ISBN # 978-1-4120-0539-6

Excerpts from *Messages from the Hollow Earth:*

Trees and Cetaceans Are Both Stewards

The trees are Majestic Beings, evolved beyond anything your thoughts can picture. They wait for you to recognize them also as the stewards of the land, as the Cetaceans are the stewards of the sea, always giving you the oxygen you need, and absorbing the pollutants you create.

And what do you do in return for this gift of life? You cut them down, you move them out of your way, and you ignore them.

They are yearning to communicate with you, yearning to feel your touch and embrace you in their love and energy. Go to them, talk to them, sit with them, as they stand vigilant over your homes and communities as protectors of your very lives. Talk to them, and they will answer. They have been waiting eons to have humans reconnect to them again.

Our Inner Earth Oceans Are Sanctuaries to All Marine Life

The Inner Earth's Oceans contain all of the life that's in the upper oceans, and more. Our oceans are teeming with life, and all of the marine forms live in harmony with one another.

All are on a vegetarian diet and do not hunt others. All live in harmony. All the marine life is very evolved compared to the life in the surface oceans. All are used to the peace and safety of our waters, and all are accessible to us. We all communicate directly to the Cetaceans and fish, and live cooperatively and in peace with one another.

Since we are all on a vegetarian diet, we don't hunt the Whales, go fishing, or farm shrimp. Therefore, Mother Nature is free to evolve in our oceans, and our oceans are sanctuaries to all ocean life. We just call to whomever we want to talk to, and they swim to our shores and converse with us. It would seem truly magical to you, but to us it is commonplace. Remember, all of us in the Hollow Earth know we are ONE.

There are numerous underwater caverns, where we go "scuba" diving and explore the intricacies and complexities of life beneath the oceans. There are so many different kinds of organisms and plants and corals that are hidden in the ocean caverns that are beauteous to see. We love to dive and swim, explore and commune with the nature elementals in the oceans. There's a whole other civilization beneath our seas that we live in peace and cooperative partnership with. How wonderful to exist in a climate of peaceful exchange that we have forged beneath the Earth.

Your surface Whales and Dolphins sometimes swim through the underground ocean tunnels to visit and commune with us. They stay a short while and then return to the surface. They wish they could stay longer, but know their mission is above ground, and hesitatingly leave for the great swim upwards.

The message on the next page is from
Dianne's future book:

TREE TALK

"**T**aking **R**esponsibility for the **E**arth and **E**nvironment"

We Are All ONE

A Note from the Author to "Hug a Tree"

Our Dear Readers,

Just as the Cetaceans are the Earth's Record Keepers living in the Oceans, do you know that the TREES are the Record Keepers living on Land?

The Trees comprise a "vast underground communication network" system that transmits information so that all Trees, everywhere on Earth, know instantly all that occurs. They are Living Libraries embodied in bark that we, as humans, can easily "tap" into (note the term "tap root"—we can tap into their vast library). Their "line" is always open to us, so tap into it—they are eagerly awaiting our call. They are waiting for us to acknowledge them as the **TREE PEOPLE.**

For uncensored worldwide news and answers to any question, Hug a Tree—it not only saves paper, but their lives as well.

We Trees Are Record Keepers

We are the Trees. We, too, are Record Keepers. Our branches are layered with information. Our leaves are recording plates that capture your words and actions as you walk by.

You can talk to us and we will record your words, even your nuances of speech. It is like turning a dial on a recording device and you talk into it. We are better than that, since we don't run on technology—it is built into us.

Our leaves look thin to your eyes, yet hold volumes of information that appears automatically to you in vision and sound when you "switch on" to us. We are self-contained books holding the records of the Earth. As our leaves sway to and fro in the wind we are sweeping the ethers and picking up pertinent information that is necessary to sustain life. It is all encoded, and you can easily break the code. We can answer any question you ask, if you just learn to hear us. We speak loud and clear to your heart—not your ear.

We Trees comprise a vast underground communications network that records all events and is privy to all that is about to occur. **If you want to know what is going to happen anywhere on Earth, just stand next to one of us, put your hand on our trunk, and ask your question. We will answer.**

We trees are guardians—sentinels stationed on Earth to serve here along with you in partnership as caretakers. We are encoded with cosmic intelligence and graced by the Divine just as you are—only we are aware of our gifts and use them to create only harmony.

You can read us as we read you—you are a Living Library and can turn the pages within your soul to access all there is to know. It is built into you…it is you. This is why your DNA is so sought after and you have been so tampered with. You are a prize worth capturing, but no one can duplicate you. With all their technology they still cannot figure you out. Only the Creator knows the code.

About the Author

Dianne Robbins is a telepath and empath, so not only does she receive information but she also feels what Lolita, Corky, Keiko, and the other Cetaceans feel. She is an Interspecies Communicator, specializing in raising people's awareness of the continuing inhumane killing of Cetaceans and the imprisonment of their species. She is of Cetacean lineage and consciousness, and has been a telepathic channel for the Cetaceans in other lifetimes. Channeling under the name LAILEL, today, she is one of the Cetaceans' voices to the world.

Dianne has always been connected to the Cetaceans, and was an active member of Greenpeace in the 1970s, only at that time, she didn't realize that she could hear them. Being telepathically linked to the Cetaceans in previous lifetimes, it was easy for her to connect with them now, once she realized that she could do this. They had been waiting for some time for her to realize this, and planted many signs along her path to call her attention to them.

In the late 1980s Dianne started her search with the questions "Who am I, why am I here, and what am I supposed to be doing?" She spent hours each day for many years in meditation and silence, out in nature, walking, and just sitting quietly to find the answers to her questions, and started receiving telepathic messages from the Cetaceans in the early 1990s. Many of the messages in this book were channeled while Dianne was at Deerfield Beach, Florida. She would sit alone by the ocean with pen and notebook, and telepathically call to the Cetaceans, "I am ready." They would then dictate their messages to her.

Dianne is irresistibly drawn to the ocean. She yearns to live near the ocean, and dreams of moving to Florida where her family and many Cetaceans are. Family life is very important to her, and she misses her family in Florida from whom she is separated, just as Lolita and Corky are separated from their families—only she has the freedom to visit her family as she wishes. Dianne fervently hopes that Lolita, Corky, and all Cetaceans in captivity will be freed, so that they, too, can be with their families again; and that someday she, too, can be with hers.

Dianne can be reached at:
www.DianneRobbins.com
Whales@DianneRobbins.com
585-802-4530

Photo and Artwork Credits

Much heartfelt gratitude for:

Page 1 & front cover: Orca – photo by Eccoblue
3: Blue Whale – Anon. (Anonymous from Internet)
4: Keiko – Anon.
11, 15: Dolphin – Max Harris
17, 20: Hawaiian Dolphins – Matisha, songofhome.com
22, 25: Orcas – Anon.
27: Hawaiian Dolphins – Matisha, songofhome.com
31: Dolphin with Jennifer Davies-North
34: Hawaiian Dolphins – Matisha
35: Gray Whale – NOAA (National Oceanic & Atmospheric Administration)
37: Orcas – Jan Daly
41: Corky – Kelly Keagy-Bullock
43: Corky and friend – Kelly Keagy-Bullock
49, 51, 52: Corky – Alexandra Morton
56: Corky – Brad
59, 63: Lolita – Peter Pijpelink
65: Lolita – Mandy H.
66: Lolita – Peter Pijpelink
69: Keiko – Anon.
74, 76: Keiko – Free Willy / Keiko Foundation
80: Orca porpoising – Minette Layne
81: Right Whale – Anon.
85: N. Atlantic Right Whale – NOAA
88: Right Whale – NOAA
90: N. Pacific Right Whale – NOAA
93: Whales with tanker – NOAA
95: Right Whale – NOAA
97, 98, 99, 100: Dolphins – Max Harris
103: Pacific White Sided Dolphins – NOAA
104: Vaquita Porpoise – NOAA
105: Orca calf and mother – Dave Ellifrit / Center for Whale Research, whaleresearch.com
107: "Mothers Love" – Daniel B. Holeman, AwakenVisions.com
108: "Newborn" – Janet Biondi
110: Humpback Whale breaching – Brett Atkins
111: Orca breaching – Courtney Smith / Center for Whale Research, whaleresearch.com
113: Orca spyhopping – Traci Walter / Center for Whale Research, whaleresearch.com
115: Orca breaching – Stefan Jacobs / Center for Whale Research, whaleresearch.com
118: "Memories" – Carlos D. Aleman, Dolphin Art Gallery

Dolphin photos on pages 17, 20, 27, 34, 135, 141, 147, 189, 193:
copyright © 2004 - 2007 Matisha (www.SongofHome.com)
Matisha is an adventure guide in Hawaii, who introduces people to wild dolphins
and whales through his sensitive inter-species programs, Ecstatic Dolphin Journeys.
His dolphin DVD, "Dolphinfinity," is an echanting interspecies dance with wild
dolphins. As a singer/songwriter/performer he presents at many retreats in Hawaii
and around the world. His website hosts the largest internet collection of dolphin
photographs in the world.

The messages in this book contain Spiritual Truths
for the elevation of human consciousness.
SPIRITUAL TRUTH IS FREE: It is our birthright.

ISBN 142516222-3

9 781425 162221